# *The*
# LITTLE BOOK OF
# PHILOSOPHY

T0385175

*Rachel Poulton*

summersdale

THE LITTLE BOOK OF PHILOSOPHY

An Hachette UK Company
www.hachette.co.uk

Summersdale Publishers Ltd
Part of Octopus Publishing Group Limited
Carmelite House
50 Victoria Embankment
LONDON
EC4Y 0DZ
UK

www.summersdale.com

Printed and bound in Poland

ISBN: 978-1-78685-808-5

# CONTENTS

# *Introduction*

## WHAT IS PHILOSOPHY?

Mention philosophy to most people and the image that springs to their mind might be one of professors stroking long beards while pondering unanswerable questions. It's often seen as a lofty discipline; a bit stuffy and inaccessible. But philosophy is simply a quest for wisdom and knowledge; *philosophia* in Ancient Greek literally means "love of wisdom". The aim of philosophy is to ask and explore life's big questions in order to help us work out what we should do and how we can live a good life. Philosophical enquiry is all about wanting to *understand* something rather than just to know it; it's active – you *do* philosophy. And, in a world of fake news and fake "facts", embarking on a quest for truth couldn't be more important. Engaging in philosophy teaches us that passively scrolling through social media feeds and passively consuming information are not the answers. We should be busy asking questions and fully exploring the answers: *enjoying* the journey as much as the destination.

Philosophers are dynamic thinkers. They have been asking questions for thousands of years and through argument and reasoning they aim to come to conclusions that, hopefully, bring greater understanding and clarity. Questions such as: What is the meaning of life? Who am I? Am I free?

Given the sheer size of the subject it would be impossible to cover every aspect of philosophy here, but this book aims to take you on a whistle-stop tour through time and thought, touching upon the most important and fascinating philosophers and their ideas – ideas that have shaped Western thought for the past 2,000 years. We will journey to Ancient Greece, the birthplace of Western philosophy, take in a bit of Eastern philosophy, and then move on to the Medieval and Renaissance periods. An exploration of modern philosophy will bring us into the twentieth century, and postmodern philosophy will conclude our trip.

At first glance, philosophy can appear overwhelming: a vast sea of enquiry and knowledge. You can pretty much philosophize about anything: education, religion, science, language, feminism – the list goes on. But by the time you've finished this book, you should know your Metaphysics from your Epistemology, your Political philosophy from your Ethics, and you should be able to distinguish between Rationalism and Empiricism. You should also have a basic understanding of the main schools of philosophy and the key thinkers – a jumping-off point from which you can then conduct your own deeper thinking in the areas that interest you. Most of all, my hope is that you finish this book with a new-found curiosity and a love of wisdom of your own.

# Pre-Socratic Philosophy

For thousands of years philosophers have been attempting to come up with rational and reasonable answers to life's big questions. But where did it all start? To answer this, we need to go back over 2,500 years to around the sixth century BCE, to a group of original thinkers known as the Pre-Socratics (so-called because they came before that Titan of philosophy, Socrates).

Socrates would be concerned with *how* we should live, but before he arrived on the scene, the very first philosophers focused on the material nature of things: what are the Earth and space made from, and what is the fundamental nature of things? Not content with the accepted mythical and supernatural explanations of the time, the Pre-Socratics started to focus on what they sensed and experienced around them. They were the first to look for rational and logical explanations of the universe, instead of relying on the metaphorical teachings embodied in the myths and legends surrounding pagan gods.

They saw instead that the world was governed by rules – that it was ordered and logical, and something that could be studied and understood. These early philosophical thinkers each had different ideas, but the four elements – water, air, fire and earth – featured heavily in their theories of why things were so.

**Thales** (624–546 BCE – see page 10) was considered the very first philosopher; he was from the Milesian school of thought. He lived on the Mediterranean, surrounded by water, so his theory that water was the basis of everything is understandable. **Anaximander** (610–546 BCE), a student of Thales, couldn't work out how some things – fire, for instance – could be made up of water. He had observed the four elements and saw them as unstable and opposed to each other – water puts out fire, so how could any one of these physical elements be the basis of all things? Instead, he suggested that the universe and everything within (the *kosmos*) had come into existence when separated from "the unbounded", or *apeiron*. This *apeiron* is not a substance; it's something mysterious, eternal and boundless. Anaximander believed everything was created from the *apeiron* and, when destroyed, would return there.

His student **Anaximenes** (585–528 BCE) disagreed with Anaximander's metaphysical theories. He observed that air could be transformed into various substances – it can be condensed to form cloud, further condensed to form water, even more condensed it becomes earth and at its most dense it becomes stone. In its less dense, or rarefied forms, air can be wind or fire. He thus concluded that air was the underlying element in all things.

Although all three theories sound pretty crazy, given our scientific knowledge these days, philosophical and scientific enquiry had begun. These early thinkers were observing the world around them, challenging the idea that the world and *kosmos* were created by gods, and attempting to explain the complexity and variability of all that surrounds us. They were engaged in rational enquiry.

# THALES
## 624–546 BCE

Thales of Miletus was a wealthy and well-travelled Greek living in the affluent city of Miletus in modern-day Turkey by the Mediterranean Sea. He is considered the first real philosopher and therefore the founder of Greek and Western philosophy. He was also a businessman, an engineer, a mathematician, a politician and an astronomer. Thales' philosophical and mathematical enquiry drew on the wisdom of Egypt and Babylonia; it is thought he travelled to Egypt where he discovered he could calculate the height of a pyramid by measuring the length of its shadow. His geometrical theorems were based on ideas from the Egyptians and Babylonians.

Like most of the Pre-Socratic philosophers, what little we know about his life and philosophy comes from later accounts (many from Aristotle), and it is difficult to determine much about his life or exactly what his theories were, but we do have some ideas. In his book *Metaphysics*,

Aristotle claimed that Thales was the first to suggest that all matter originates with one single element.

Thales believed water was the main giver of life and observed how it could change into mist, ice, liquid and earth, and so his theory was that the underlying principle of the world was water. He believed the world was a disc that floated on water, and that phenomena such as earthquakes could be explained logically as the result of waves moving the Earth around. Although wrong, Thales' theory was groundbreaking because it marked the beginnings of rational enquiry and challenged the supernatural thinking of the day. Before this, people looked to the gods for answers, believing that it was restless or angry gods who had created the Earth and who were causing the quakes.

As an astrologer, Thales is said to have predicted when the solar eclipse of 585 BCE would occur, as well as working out how long a year was and when equinoxes and solstices would happen. His fascination with the stars is said to have led to an unfortunate accident that Aesop (a slave and storyteller who lived in Ancient Greece around 620–564 BCE) told a fable about: "The Astrologer who Fell into a Well". It is said that one night Thales was so busy gazing up at the heavens that he stumbled into a well, only to be rescued by an old woman who remarked that he would do better to keep his eyes on earthly matters, rather than the mysteries of the skies. How lucky for the world of philosophy and science that he managed to do both.

# PYTHAGORAS
## c.570–495 BCE

One of the most well-known Pre-Socratics, Pythagoras believed that numbers lay at the centre of all things. His ideas influenced Plato, Aristotle and Western esotericism. Much of what we know about Pythagoras is, as with most of the Pre-Socratics, open to conjecture and built around myth and legend. He is said to have been the incarnation of the god Apollo, to have had a golden thigh and a magic arrow, and to be able to be in two places at one time. You can see why he was such a legend.

He theorized that the planets and stars move according to a harmonious mathematical relationship and produce an inaudible symphony known as the "music of the spheres". He is also well-known for his theory of *metempsychosis* – a belief in the transmigration of the soul (that when the body dies, the soul lives on, passing to another body, either human or animal).

Pythagoras set up a commune of followers in Croton, southern Italy. Life in the Pythagorean community focused on improving the soul, ready for "the next life", and was built on the principles of extreme ascetism (self-discipline and denial of pleasures often for spiritual or religious reasons), equality, vegetarianism (although beans were banned), a love of music as a connection to the divine, and a dedication to developing the psyche.

# HERACLITUS

## c.535–475 BCE

Another Pre-Socratic with radical ideas, Heraclitus believed that fire was the fundamental element. He believed that from fire came everything else and that the *kosmos* (an organized universe) exists in a constant state of flux. According to Heraclitus, everything is constantly changing and transforming but is also interconnected and underpinned by a hidden order called *Logos* (*Logos* being divine reason).

Heraclitus is famous for his deliberately confusing writing (he was pretty elitist and thought only the learned should be able to fathom his teachings); his book *On Nature* is filled with puns and paradoxes that are left wide open to interpretation. Take this notable saying: "We step and do not step into the same rivers; we are and are not", which illustrates his belief that everything changes around us and that all things in the world are always in motion, but, perplexingly, suggests that although things change, they stay the same. If we stick with the river metaphor, we might interpret his saying as: although the water is flowing around us and continuously changing, the river stays the same; parts of things change but the whole remains the same.

Heraclitus also argued for the unity of opposites: "What is at variance agrees with itself." It's the balancing of opposite tensions that bring about harmony, and it is from this tension, or strife, that all things come into being. Hot becomes cold, war becomes peace. He believed everything is always changing, is always "becoming", and a universal law of justice will always balance things out. Heraclitus believed that in order to live well we should become aware of our oneness and live according to the flow of nature.

# PARMENIDES
## c.515–450s BCE

Another highly influential Pre-Socratic philosopher, Parmenides, completely disagreed with Heraclitus' theory of the *kosmos* being in constant flux, with everything perpetually changing. He argued that the world was "one being", which was static and unchanging, and that the only thing that exists was reality itself. He believed that his philosophy, which he wrote down in an epic poem called *On Nature*, of which only fragments have survived, was relayed to him via a goddess.

In the poem he distinguished between two views of reality – sensory perception, or "The Way of Appearance/ Opinion", and reasoned reality, or "The Way of Truth". He explained that we can only ever think or talk of things that exist, something *that is*, and all we can say of it is that *it exists*. This is "The Way of Truth". He argued that we cannot conceive or talk about *what is not* and believed it was impossible for things that are *not* to become things that *are*, so things cannot exist in the past or the future because neither the past nor the future actually exist. Following this thinking – that one cannot conceive of what doesn't exist – he concluded that the only thing that exists is *what is* now, a present that is eternal and unchanging.

It's confusing stuff and riddled with inaccuracies, but what is significant is that Parmenides is using logic and language to come up with his theory of being. He is using reasoning over sensory experience to say what reality is.

In the second part of *On Nature*, Parmenides considered "The Way of Opinion". He explained that any movement or changes we see are simply down to perception and are obtained through the senses, which are not reliable.

Heraclitus' theory of "becoming" and Parmenides' theory of "being", although flawed and somewhat confusing, mark the beginnings of metaphysical thinking, and both philosophers are seen as the founders of **ontology** (the branch of Metaphysics that focuses on being, existence and reality). Parmenides was tackling the philosophical problem of reality versus perception and discussing the concept of being – what exists and what doesn't. He had a huge influence on Plato (and therefore Western philosophy) – Plato even wrote a dialogue, "Parmenides", after him.

As we have seen, philosophical thought and enquiry was developing; the Pre-Socratic bid to understand the material nature of the universe had led to metaphysical theories of *what* reality is and *how* we should perceive the universe.

# ATOMISM

Atomism originated in the fifth century BCE with two philosophers: **Leucippus of Miletus** (dates unknown) and **Democritus** (*c.*460–*c.*370 BCE). The main idea in atomism is that the universe and everything in it consists of two things: atoms and the void. The word atom comes from the Greek, *atomon*, meaning "uncuttable" or "indivisible"; an atom is the smallest, impenetrable part of any chemical element. Unlike our current definition of an atom, the atoms in this theory are all different shapes and sizes and are ricocheting around a void.

According to atomism, all things that exist come into being when atoms collide and combine within the void. The different objects we see and perceive are determined by the kind of atoms that make each object up and the way those differently shaped atoms move and come together. Atomism attempted to reconcile Heraclitus' theory of ever-changing flux with Parmenides' ideas that everything is eternal and static, that there is no material change and that all change is mere illusion.

Atomists take a decidedly materialist and determinist (the philosophical idea that events and choices are determined by previous causes) view of the world; everything in the universe is made up of atoms and exists as a result of strict causal, physical laws.

# METAPHYSICS

The word "metaphysics" comes from the Greek, meaning "after the study of the natural". It is thought it was later used by a first-century editor who brought together a number of Aristotle's writings under the title *Metaphysics*, which came after his other work entitled *Physics* – *meta* means "after", so it's literally "after *Physics*". It is the branch of philosophy that deals with existence and the nature of reality – how things come to *be*. It tackles the more abstract concepts of being, knowing, identity and change, time and space. As time and philosophical thinking has moved on, some aspects of Metaphysics have become areas of study in themselves – philosophy of mind, for instance, is a huge area still linked to Metaphysics. Metaphysics asks questions like: What is reality? What is everything made of? Do things exist, or are they just ideas and projections of the mind? Does God exist? Why is there something rather than nothing?

Metaphysics is concerned with asking what anything is caused by, and with tracking the creation of things back to the "First Cause". Aristotle theorized that there was something at the very beginning of the universe that was not caused by anything else, and he believed that that "something" was God.

When Parmenides said, "Being is; not being is not", he was thinking metaphysically. He was questioning the nature of reality – what actually exists versus the world that man observes with his senses.

Empiricists (philosophers who take a more scientific, evidence-based approach to the study of human knowledge) are sceptical of most Metaphysical claims because they generally cannot be tested and proven.

## The Big Three:

# SOCRATES, PLATO AND ARISTOTLE

# SOCRATES
## c.470–399 BCE

Socrates, the first of our "Big Three" philosophers, was born around 470 BCE, and lived in Athens during the city-state's cultural Golden Age. He was revolutionary in that he moved philosophical thinking away from the Pre-Socratic obsession with asking questions about the material world and toward more ethical considerations – he wanted to know how people could live good, moral lives.

By all accounts he wasn't a particularly attractive man: he was short, fat and bald with a squashed nose and a personal hygiene problem. Despite good intentions, he was also very irritating, randomly questioning his fellow Athenian citizens in the streets and markets in an attempt to get people thinking more carefully and actively. Socrates is famous for declaring that "the only thing I know is that I know nothing". He wanted people to find out the true meaning of things and not just accept what they heard or even said themselves. Rather than coming up with answers and telling people what *he* believed, he thought that the best way of getting to the truth was to keep asking questions.

Socrates' way of exploring ideas through questioning became known as the Socratic method. For him, the most important thing was that people got to know themselves and that they learned to understand their soul. He believed that once you know yourself you can live a life that is true to you. The Socratic method allows us to find out what we think, what we believe and who we are – by asking questions, reasoning, talking, and teasing out answers, we can get to know ourselves a little better.

Socrates didn't write anything down, so we know about him only through other people's accounts – most notably those of Plato, who was one of his students and who wrote down his ideas in the form of dialogues or philosophical discussions. In Plato's dialogues, which incorporate exciting characters and lively discussions, Socrates is almost always the star, and the conversation revolves around him and some sort of conceptual question, such as "What is love?" or "What makes a 'good' life?" Socrates believed that, in order to experience love, you have to know what love is. In order to live a "good" life you have to know what virtue is.

And, for Socrates, virtue is knowledge: to truly know is to be truly good. He didn't think people did bad things because they were bad; he thought that they did them because they simply didn't know any better. He felt that if people really understood what it is to be good, and to choose virtuous actions, then they would never choose to do evil – especially if they knew how much it would hurt themselves and others. Basically, he believed all human evil was a result of ignorance, and that if people would just question what they were doing they would always do the right thing.

So, for Socrates, a life of philosophical contemplation working out all these important things was the best way to live. He wasn't interested in fame, power, money or possessions, but truly believed a good life should be spent pursuing the truth. This is what he meant when he famously said, "the unexamined life is not worth living".

With all this encouraging people to think for themselves, ask questions and challenge authority, you can imagine the

Athenian leaders were none too pleased with Socrates. He was keen to get citizens questioning all long-held beliefs, but in particular the idea of democracy and the Athenian state's practice of justice. He was therefore seen as a threat to the state and, in 399 BCE, was charged with impiety (or irreverence, for not believing in the gods of the state) and with corrupting the youth. Plato's *Apology* describes the trial and how Socrates defended himself. He was found guilty of his crimes and, despite having a chance of paying a fine or escaping prison with a bribe, Socrates chose to obey the law of Athens and to drink a poisonous brew of hemlock. His execution was devastating for his friends and followers, but he reassured them, "all of philosophy is training for death". For Socrates, philosophy really was a matter of life and death.

# THE SOCRATIC METHOD

During the fifth century BCE the "social gadfly", Socrates, set about unsettling Athenian society and politics with probing questioning. His aim was "to sting people and whip them into a fury, all in the service of truth" (from Plato's *Apology*). He was engaging people in the Socratic method: a form of philosophical enquiry based upon rigorous, systematic questioning to stimulate critical thinking. Socrates engaged his fellow Athenians in cooperative, argumentative dialogue in order to challenge their long-held or underlying beliefs.

The aim wasn't to persuade or convince, or to put forward emotional or rhetorical defences, but to get closer to the truth by logically eliminating contradictory viewpoints. It was generally a collaborative process with ideas building upon ideas.

In the Platonic dialogues, characters discuss a philosophical problem in order to reveal the truth of an issue. They are engaging, enlightening, dramatic, and sometimes funny, but the words of Socrates always aimed to challenge and bring greater understanding.

# ETHICS

The field of Ethics deals with moral principles. It's the branch of philosophy that organizes, defends and addresses right and wrong conduct. Also referred to as moral philosophy, Ethics is concerned with what is good for individuals and society. It attempts to define concepts such as good and evil, right and wrong, crime and justice, virtue and vice, and broadly asks, "How should we live?"

Ethics comes from the Greek word *ēthikós*, which means "relating to one's character"; the root word *ethos* means "character, moral nature". The term virtue ethics is used to describe the Ethical philosophies of Socrates and Aristotle, who believed individual character was the driving force behind ethical actions. For Socrates, knowledge and virtue go hand in hand and for Aristotle, acting virtuously, doing the right thing, leads to happiness, so virtue equals happiness.

Modern philosophy distinguishes between three types of Ethics: meta-ethics, normative ethics and applied ethics. Meta-ethics deals with the nature of moral judgement – for instance, what are the origins and meanings of ethical principles? Normative ethics is concerned with how people should act, from a moral viewpoint. And applied ethics tackles big concepts such as war, animal rights, abortion or capital punishment.

# PLATO
## c.428–348 BCE

Plato, our second behemoth of philosophy, was a student of Socrates and teacher of Aristotle, so his influence is enormous. Indeed, it was said by the philosopher and mathematician, Alfred North Whitehead, that all Western philosophy is "a series of footnotes to Plato". He not only laid the foundations for Western philosophy and science, but also impacted mathematics, political philosophy, early Christianity and spirituality.

Plato was born into a wealthy and politically influential family in Athens in 428 BCE and, as a young man, became a devoted follower of Socrates. Most of what we know about Socrates' philosophical ideas and practice comes from Plato's writings about him, which are referred to as Plato's dialogues. With Socrates appearing as the main character, the early dialogues are said really to reflect Socrates' philosophical concerns, while the middle and later dialogues illustrate Plato's own theories on life, the universe and everything. Like Socrates, he was a lover of wisdom and dedicated his life to seeking the truth.

Plato travelled to Egypt and Italy, and was influenced by the Pythagoreans he met in Sicily who convinced him of the importance of numbers and introduced him to the ideas of a transmigrating soul and afterlife. After his travels, he returned to Athens to open the Academy, the world's first university dedicated to the pursuit of knowledge. The aim of the Academy was to study philosophy, science and mathematics in order to improve life in the Greek city states. It was at the Academy where he met and taught Aristotle, another philosophical Titan of Greece's Golden Age.

Plato's philosophical range was extensive – he was concerned with Metaphysics, epistemology (see page 40), ethics, politics, philosophy of mind, language, religion and aesthetics. He wrote about the soul, the arts, and virtues such as courage, justice, wisdom and piety. He wrote about the state and governance, love and friendship. He explored nature through physics and chemistry, and studied physiology and medicine.

In his Theory of Forms or Theory of Ideas (an idea that most scholars think is mostly Plato's rather than Socrates'), Plato distinguishes between a physical external world that is perceived with our eyes and senses and an abstract world of perfect Ideas or Forms that can only be accessed by the mind. Like Parmenides, he was grappling with the differences between appearance and reality, opinion and truth. Plato was influenced by Heraclitus' theory that things are constantly changing or "becoming" and are therefore difficult to define. Parmenides on the other hand believed changes to be illusory and that everything is in a static state of "being". Through his Theory of Forms, Plato was saying that both philosophers were right – the world we see and live in is ever-changing and temporary and is made up of copies of an immutable perfect Form that resides in some transcendent realm. True knowledge is permanent and found in clearly defined Forms. So, to truly know anything we have to understand the perfect Form, the perfect idea of everything. Plato thought philosophers were best suited to think in this abstract way and understand the Forms; he thought ordinary people were too dependent on their senses and on appearances, and that reality lay *beyond* appearances and required deep philosophical thinking to uncover it.

Things can be clearly defined in the world of "being" because they are unchanging and permanent, and for Plato all knowledge exists here, so "knowledge" can therefore be said to be permanent. In *The Republic*, Plato has Socrates explain the world of illusion and the world of reality through the literary device of allegory.

Imagine, if you will, a group of prisoners who have been chained up all their lives in a cave. All they can see is a wall. Behind them is a great fire that casts shadows of people, animals and objects onto the wall. These shadows are their reality; it's all they know. However, one day a prisoner breaks free and tentatively moves out of the cave, where he looks up to a great sun and sees how it casts light upon the real objects, so much more magnificent and perfect than the shadows: everything is illuminated. When he returns to the cave, the others don't believe what he has seen – they think he is foolish and mad, and they have no desire to look up.

The cave is our world. What Plato is saying is that we are all trapped in this world of "becoming", where everything is illusory and in a state of flux. Outside the cave, the realm of "being" is where true meaning resides, and we can discover it if we turn to philosophy, understand the Forms and uncover the truth, which is illuminated by sunlight.

Plato believed that an individual's soul accesses the realm of Forms before birth. Through his Pythagorean belief in metempsychosis (the transmigration of the soul into another living being after death), he explains that it is the soul that holds true knowledge learned in the World of Forms; before we are reborn our souls visit the World of Forms and contemplate all these perfect ideas. We therefore have all the knowledge within us; we just need to ask the right questions in order to reveal or recollect it. This is what Socrates' aim was in urging us to turn to philosophy to reveal the real truth – otherwise we will be forever locked into a world of illusion.

In a number of dialogues, including *The Republic* and *The Laws*, Plato considers the state and sets out his political ideals. He talks of a very hierarchical structure of society, with the perfect state being made up of a thinking elite (philosophers, basically, or rulers), soldiers who are there for defence, and, beneath the soldiers, the workers. The rulers should immerse themselves in philosophy in order to govern from a position of wisdom and reason. He believed successful states are based on an aristocracy, with a philosopher-king as head. These philosopher-kings would be lovers of truth and wisdom, look toward the light, know the highest good and be incorruptible by money or power – good luck with that then!

His political philosophy was very totalitarian. Despite Athenian attempts at democracy at the time, Plato didn't believe the common man to be worthy of the vote because, as seen with his Forms, they just couldn't access the knowledge. He also would have banned art, again with reference to the Forms, on the grounds that art is a false representation of perfect Forms, and so it is a waste of time. I'm not sure living in a Platonic state would have been that much fun.

Plato's philosophical enquiry was indeed prolific, and we've barely scratched the surface here. His death was not as dramatic as Socrates' (he is said to have simply died in his sleep), but his life, like that of Socrates, was one of relentless examination. Following on from the groundwork Socrates laid, Plato taught us how to *do* philosophy, and raised the questions that we still ponder 2,500 years later – and that have made our lives much richer.

# EPISTEMOLOGY

Epistemology is the branch of philosophy that deals with the theory of knowledge. The word comes from the Greek *episteme* meaning "knowledge" and *logos* meaning "logical discourse". It's about exploring the nature of knowledge, and how it's acquired and shared. The onus is on distinguishing between justified belief and opinion. Questions Epistemologists might ask are: What does it mean to say that we *know* something? What is knowledge? How do we know what we know? How is knowledge acquired?

When considering how knowledge is acquired philosophers talk of *a priori* and *a posteriori* knowledge. *A priori* knowledge is gained through deduction and requires only the use of reason: it's things that we know already, that are self-evident, like the colour red, sisters being female siblings, and basic mathematics. Then there is *a posteriori* or empirical knowledge that can only be known by experiencing it or through scientific experiment. Knowing that my cup of tea is hot requires me to experience the tea as hot and therefore counts as *a posteriori* knowledge. All knowledge or justified beliefs are derived from *a priori* or *a posteriori* knowledge.

# ARISTOTLE
## c.384–322 BCE

Aristotle is the third of our "Big Three" philosophers. Born around 384 BCE in northern Greece, at the age of 17 he went to Athens to study at Plato's Academy, and ended up staying for 20 years, first as Plato's student and then as a teacher. He went on to tutor Alexander the Great (considered the greatest military leader that ever lived, Alexander conquered most of the known world and created the largest empire the world had seen until then) before setting up his own school in Athens called the Lyceum. His teaching was called *peripatetic* because he liked to walk around the grounds as he taught students how to think, reason and discuss.

Aristotle never stopped asking questions, including ones pertinent to everyday life and to being human. He asked things like: What is art for? What are friends for? What makes people happy? His answer to this last question lay in finding a golden mean; he believed that living a balanced, virtuous life without too many extremes would lead to the Good Life or, in Greek, *eudaimonia*, which means "flourishing".

In his *Nicomachean Ethics* (Nicomachus was his son and the book was dedicated to him), Aristotle said, "happiness depends upon ourselves". He meant that no one else can make you happy or unhappy, but if you are honest, friendly, courageous, honourable, generous and healthy, and you keep learning, you are bound to live a happy life.

Aristotle worked out four aspects of human nature that he believed, in order to flourish, you had to have balance in. What he claimed wasn't rocket science, but is worth a look:

1. Because we are physical beings, we have to care for our bodies by eating well, exercising regularly and resting when we are tired. Find a healthy balance and you'll physically flourish.

2. We should try to find emotional balance too, making sure we avoid things that make us unhappy and do more of the things that make us feel good.

3. As human beings we do best in groups, so living and socializing with others is really important for individual happiness.

4. Possibly the most important aspect of human nature is our ability to learn, create and express ourselves. We will flourish if we follow our interests and keep learning and exploring new things.

Aristotle's contribution to *Metaphysics* was to break away from his teacher, Plato, and insist that matter and form was something very tangible, as opposed to Plato's idea that there was a transcendent, idealized version of everything (see Plato's Theory of Forms, page 35). Aristotle believed that reality was here and now, and that there were clear and unequivocal ways to define what was in front of us.

To show how we can always define the things around us, Aristotle said that everything has "four causes": firstly, there's the *material* cause – what something is actually made from – for example, "this table is made out of wood". Then there is the *formal* cause – this is what form that material takes. In the table example, we know that this table is a table because it has four legs that hold up the top, and the shape and arrangement of the bits of wood take the form of a table. The third cause, called the *efficient* cause, refers to the maker of the thing – so in this case, the furniture maker is the efficient cause of the table. The final cause is the thing's *purpose*; everything is partly what it is because of its purpose. We can therefore know without doubt that this is a table, even if the particular table in question is an unconventional one, because it was intended to be a table, is made out of table materials, and is used as a table. This theory is rooted firmly in the material world around us, yet was groundbreaking in Aristotle's day.

Aristotle also established the science of *logic* and gave the world a logical system for working out truths. He came up with the idea of deductive inference by using something called a syllogism – an inference made up of two propositions and a conclusion. For example: "All men are mortal; Greeks are men; therefore, Greeks are mortal". If both premises are true, then you can deduce your conclusion. It's the same approach that Sherlock Holmes would take when solving a case.

Aristotle's development of logical argument and his empirical approach to the natural sciences gave us the blueprint for rationality. Aristotle was considered one of the greatest men who ever lived, and the grandfather of science. His theories and ideas have influenced Islamic thought as well as Christian theology and have impacted nearly every area of study including physics, biology, zoology, geography, poetry, politics and government, theatre, music and ethics.

# SCEPTICISM

When Socrates professed he knew nothing, he was exhibiting sceptical tendencies. The Sceptics are a group of philosophers who believe that absolute, certain knowledge is impossible. Proponents argue convincingly both for and against a particular proposition – a bit like having an argument with yourself. Through rigorous examination of all arguments for and against any proposition, Sceptics have come to the conclusion that nothing can be known with absolute certainty, especially when it comes to controversial questions such as: Does God exist? Or, Is there life after death?

The oldest school of Scepticism began with the philosopher, **Pyrrho** (*c.*360–*c.*270 BCE). He is supposed to have travelled to India with Alexander the Great's army and, after talking with sages there, returned to Greece completely "chilled out" and decided to suspend judgement on everything. He found peace or *ataraxia* (a state of *ataraxia* meant you were free from worry and anxiety) in having no opinion on anything and believing nothing to be either true or false.

Nowadays to have a sceptical attitude is to be doubtful of the truth of something, a direct nod to Pyrrho and his "whatever" attitude. Scepticism has gone in and out of fashion throughout history. The Romans weren't keen, and knowledge of it disappeared during the Middle Ages, but when the Ancient texts were translated into Latin during the Renaissance and Reformation, people took an interest in Scepticism again. René Descartes (see page 103) is famous for attempting to challenge Scepticism by being sceptical. In *Meditations on First Philosophy* (1641) he set out to prove that absolute truths *do* exist by eliminating any uncertainty in all his enquiries. After tirelessly investigating all he knew to be true he came up with one certainty – that he is thinking, therefore he exists. So, he proved the Ancients wrong – absolute, certain knowledge is possible. Later, in the eighteenth century, the Scottish philosopher David Hume (see page 110) argued that you can't prove that anything exists beyond the mind – he was sceptical about everything.

# Eastern Philosophy

While philosophers in Ancient Greece were laying the foundations for Western philosophy as we know it, philosophical thought had also been developing in East Asia and South Asia. Throughout India, various cultural traditions and beliefs were merging together into Hinduism, now the third largest religion in the world and followed by over one billion people.

Hinduism is based on the philosophical teachings found in the Ancient Sanskrit texts known as the Vedas. In Sanskrit "Veda" means "knowledge or wisdom", and the Vedas are some of the oldest sacred texts in the world. One collection of Vedas, called The Upanishads, dates back to around 800 BCE and is concerned with ontology, or the philosophical examination of being. The Vedas are seen as "authorless", or as the words of Brahma (a god of creation in Hinduism), but many Indian theologians believe they are the result of revelations seen by sages while meditating. The Vedas set out philosophical concepts and ideas, some of which are shared with Buddhism and Jainism, two other influential Eastern philosophies originating in India. The focus of Ancient Hinduism was to understand that human suffering occurs because of ignorance, and that knowledge will liberate the individual from suffering. Hindu epistemology accepts that knowledge is gained through perception, inference, comparison, testimonies of reliable experts and realism.

Hindu philosophy is concerned with the nature and relationship between Brahman (reality), Atman (the individual soul) and Prakti (the empirical world). Unlike Buddhists who don't believe in a soul or self, Hinduism posits that the soul is permanent, transmigrational and underlies the whole world.

Jainism is a less conventional Indian philosophy that explores ideas around metaphysics, reality, cosmology, ontology, epistemology and divinity. There is a philosophical belief in mind–body dualism (that the mind and body are separable) and in the idea that there is an eternal universe. Jainists understand truth to be relative and multifaceted, and believe that all possible viewpoints can be accommodated. Jainism advocates vegetarianism and strongly promotes non-violence. Like Buddhism and Hinduism, Jainism follows the laws of karma and moksha, with moksha being a state of bliss attained once liberated from karmic bonds and the cycle of life, death and rebirth (known as nirvana in Buddhism).

# BUDDHISM

Buddhism is an Eastern philosophy based on the teachings of Siddhartha Gautama - the Buddha. He was born around 623 BCE in Nepal and grew up in a very privileged royal court, but after encountering death, pain and suffering outside the confines of his royal palace, he decided to go on a journey to find out how to reduce the amount of suffering human beings experience. He asked: How should we live?

Siddhartha explored many different ways to find the answer, but it was while meditating under a tree that he realized the way to end suffering is to change how we *think* and *react* to the negative things that we come across in life. This "light bulb" moment is referred to as Siddhartha's "enlightenment" and from then on, he was known as the Buddha, "the enlightened one". He decided that he would spend the rest of his life teaching people how to live in a more enjoyable and positive way. He believed that people should follow "the Middle Way", which is similar to Aristotle's idea that if you avoid extremes you will lead a much happier life.

The Buddha said you had to do things "right". He believed that when an act is "right", it is done by the right person, in the right place, at the right time, for the right reason, and in the right way.

Buddhists believe the path to enlightenment is through meditation, which also helps develop compassion, love, patience, generosity and forgiveness – all virtues that the Buddha's teachings encourage. The term Buddha literally means "fully awake", so it follows that in order to live a happy life people should make sure that they are always focused and consciously thinking about what they are saying and doing.

The Buddha also said it is essential to understand the three ways of being. First of all, individuals have to realize that everything is always changing and no matter how hard they try they cannot stop it. Secondly, the Buddha said that people have to accept that they will always come across difficult situations, so the best thing to do is to change how they think and react to them. This will help them to live more peacefully. Thirdly, the Buddha believed that we are all one, that to think of ourselves as separate from one another or from the universe is wrong. We must understand that we are one and therefore love and care for *all* living things.

Buddhists believe in reincarnation, the idea that everyone lives many lives. We are born, live, die and then reborn again, a process called Samsara. Whether or not you have a good life depends on your karma.

# KARMA

Karma is the Indian Sanskrit term for the law of cause and effect. According to karmic law all actions and thought bring corresponding rewards or punishments. The Christian Bible also alludes to a karmic law, "for whatsoever a man soweth, that shall he also reap". If you do good things, good things will happen and you will feel joy and happiness. If you do bad things, then bad things will happen and you will experience discontentment.

Karma tells us to take moral responsibility for our actions because it has an effect on our future lives. Each individual will experience Samsara, or rebirth and death, and thus suffering, until a state of nirvana is reached. Nirvana is the ultimate goal of humans and can be described as a state of consciousness where you are free from any suffering or desire; it's a transcendent state of profound peace and wisdom. Indian soteriologies – beliefs about salvation – say that liberation from the process of Samsara requires individuals to follow *right* views and actions in this life because their future lives depend on it. Indeed, it follows then that one's present circumstances have been influenced by the actions of one's past lives. In Indian philosophy karma serves as a moral law and the incentive to live a moral life.

# CONFUCIUS
## 551–479 BCE

Born in 551 BCE in Lu, China, Confucius was a teacher,
philosopher and political theorist. He was an ordinary man
whose teachings had an extraordinary influence on East
Asian civilization. Confucius was dedicated to learning.
From the age of 15 he sought out the best teachers and
started studying and mastering the six arts: ritual, music,
archery, charioteering, calligraphy and arithmetic – as well
as mastering poetry and history. By the time he was in his
thirties he was a brilliant teacher. He showed that, through
learning, all people, even the ordinary ones, were capable
of great wisdom and worthiness. For Confucius, education
was at the heart of his philosophy, he saw education as
a means of acquiring wisdom, building character and
transforming society.

Confucius was a great believer in looking at the past to
work out how best to live, so he considered which Chinese
traditions had endured and why, and found that traditional

values such as caring for other people, loyalty and respect for family and friends were key. He concluded that happiness and social harmony lay in developing a moral community and upholding social values and traditions. Confucianism – the way of life taught by Confucius – is more a philosophy than a religion, and it has had a profound influence on spiritual and political life in China for over 2,000 years.

Confucianism is a humanist philosophy (it doesn't focus on a god or heaven but, rather, places importance on people and society) and starts with the individual taking responsibility for their own actions. This then extends to the family. He believed in filial piety, respect for one's elders and reverence for the family, as well as believing that being a good child, parent, sibling or friend was important morally, socially and politically. Confucianism teaches that developing the self is good for society and results in a sound social order, which is the bedrock of political stability and peace.

Confucius believed it was a government's responsibility to educate people in order to reach "mutual understanding"

between government and subjects, and that leaders should lead by example, being thoroughly educated and morally incorruptible – an idea that is reminiscent of Plato's idea of the philosopher-king.

Confucianism makes family ethics a public rather than private concern, with community being key. He believed that "persons of humanity, in wishing to establish themselves, also establish others, and in wishing to enlarge themselves, also enlarge others". And at the heart of Confucianism is the Golden Rule (see opposite).

# THE GOLDEN RULE

Although the Golden Rule cannot be attributed to any particular philosophy or religion, Confucius swore by it and believed it to be central to living a good life. He urged people: "Do not do unto another that you would not have him do unto you. Thou needest this law alone. It is the foundation of all the rest." The Golden Rule has been central to social order and philosophies throughout the world and thinkers have propagated it as a moral code to live by for millennia. Aristotle said: "We should conduct ourselves toward others as we would have them act toward us." In 30 BCE, the Jewish rabbi Hillel the Elder said: "What is hateful to you, do not to your fellow men:

this is the whole truth; the rest is the explanation; go and learn." And Jesus said it too, around 30 CE: "Therefore all things whatsoever ye would that men should do to you, do ye even so to them." Though it has its pedantic critics (what if the other person has different ideas of good and bad, pain and pleasure?), at its heart, this moral principle is a bit of a no-brainer really: be kind, loving and fair toward others because that is how you would like people to behave toward you. The Golden Rule encourages personal responsibility for one's actions with regard to the people around you. It requires the individual to act with empathy, care and compassion toward others, because that is how we would hope others would act toward us.

# LAO TZU
## c. SIXTH/FIFTH CENTURY BCE

Lao Tzu, or Laozi (also known as the "Supreme Old Lord" and the somewhat Star Wars-esque "Supremely Mysterious and Primordial Emperor"), was an Ancient Chinese philosopher and writer who is said to have written the *Tao Te Ching* – the most important text in the philosophy of Taoism. It is not clear when Lao Tzu lived, or even if he existed at all, but some say he lived during the sixth to fifth centuries BCE, with Chinese legends telling numerous stories about his origins and his life. It is said he was the historian in charge of the imperial archives in the court of the Chinese Zhou Dynasty, or Zhou Kingdom, a large, powerful province in China at the time; and he is also thought to have been a contemporary of Confucius.

After growing tired of the increasing immorality and corruption in the Zhou court, it was said that he decided to leave the kingdom, but the guard asked him to write down his ideas. This collection of wise thoughts became known as the *Tao Te Ching*, sometimes referred to as *Lao Tzu*, which explains his theory of the *tao* (meaning "the way") and *te* (meaning "virtue" or "moral goodness") in a series of sayings or proverbs.

Some historians contest the authorship of the *Tao Te Ching* and argue that it was written by lots of different people and not only Lao Tzu, but, regardless of who wrote it, the book forms the basis of the Chinese school of thought known as Taoism. The most significant concept within the *Tao Te Ching* is *tao*, which literally means "road" or "way", although the book itself claims that defining *tao* is an impossible task. Loosely defined, it is the great force behind the universe, while at the same time it *is* the universe. Taoism advocates a life lived in harmony with the *tao*. To achieve this harmony, a person must adopt a state of *Wu Wei*, or "non-action" or "not forcing". One must cultivate calm, avoid aggression or violence, and not hanker after wealth or fame. Taoists believe that it is our natural state to be in harmony with *tao*, and, by following the teachings of the *Tao Te Ching*, we can return to our natural state of harmony and peace.

# Ancient Philosophy

After the "Golden Age" of Athens and the wonders explored by the classical philosophies of Socrates, Plato and Aristotle, there came a time of turmoil and chaos. With the death of Alexander the Great in 323 BCE, the empire he had amassed disintegrated into warring factions competing for land and riches. This instability paved the way for an increasingly prosperous city-state, Rome, to gain strength and power and begin creating an empire that would, at its height in about 117 CE, encompass large parts of Europe, North Africa and the Middle East. From the death of Alexander the Great and the beginnings of the Roman Empire around 31 BCE, philosophical thought was developing at a rapid pace with new ideas travelling throughout the newly established empire. Three of the most influential schools of thought in the Greco-Roman world were Epicureanism, Cynicism and Stoicism.

# EPICUREANISM

Epicureanism is a philosophical doctrine founded around 300 BCE by the Ancient Greek philosopher **Epicurus** (341–270 BCE). At the heart of Epicureanism is an emphasis on living a life that brings the greatest amount of pleasure to all concerned. Although proclaimed an immoral hedonist by his critics, Epicurus wasn't advocating a life of debauchery, but instead was suggesting that the aim of life is to reach a state of tranquillity, or *ataraxia*, and to live without fear or bodily pain – a state known as *aponia*. A combination of *ataraxia* and *aponia* brings the greatest amount of pleasure and Epicurus claimed it could be attained through moderation to avoid the dissatisfaction that excess and overindulgence can lead to.

Epicurus believed the gods existed in a space between worlds called *metakosmia*, but that they had no interest in human affairs, so people should pursue happiness without fear of retribution or judgement. He thought that our lives on this planet are short so we should enjoy ourselves – believing that our consciousness and free will were intended to allow us to pursue a life of pleasure without feeling we have to follow anyone else's doctrines.

He worked out what people needed to be happy, and it wasn't riches, status, power or even marriage. For Epicurus, the life best lived was one surrounded by friends and doing work that was fulfilling and meaningful (not because you wanted to be rich), and not working long hours that stop you spending time with people you care about. He decided the best way to live was alongside friends, so he set up a sort of commune, just outside Athens, where like-minded people came together, worked together, cared for one another, and had time each day to improve their own minds and self-understanding and to think philosophically.

Epicurus was also concerned with people's irrational fear of death. One of his theories, often called the "no subject of harm" argument, says that as we cease to exist when we die, and therefore won't have any experience of death, it is foolish to fear it or allow thoughts about death to cause us pain while we are living. Influenced by the atomists, he believed the soul was made up of tiny atoms that, when the body dies, disperse into a giant void never to be seen again. So, if that's your lot, why not focus on being the very best *you* that you can be and follow pursuits that truly make you happy?

# CYNICISM

Cynicism arose in Ancient Greece in the fourth century BCE and went on to influence thought in the Roman Empire. It originated from the ascetic ideas of the Ancient Greek philosophers Antisthenes, Diogenes the Cynic and, later on, Crates of Thebes. Central to Cynicism is to live a life of virtue in accordance with nature and to reject aspirations for wealth, possessions, social standing or power; happiness lies in simplicity and people don't need any *thing* to achieve it. The idea is to live in a way that is natural to each person and to dismiss all imposed conventions.

The Cynic chose to live completely authentically, according to their own natural instincts, rather than adhering to society's expectations. It was an anarchic "up yours" to the establishment: *"I won't do what you tell me, because what you tell me to do goes against my nature and traps me in an unhappy quest for social acceptance, status, wealth and stuff."* The Cynic's purpose was to actively challenge and renounce imposed political and social orders and live completely honestly.

One of the founders of Cynicism was **Diogenes of Sinope** (*c.*412–323 BCE) who had travelled to Athens after being exiled from Sinope (in what is now Turkey), where he was influenced by Antisthenes, a student of Socrates. Diogenes developed Socrates' idea that happiness lies in living a life of virtue rather than pleasure.

Diogenes took this to the extreme, living practically naked in a barrel on the streets of Athens, free of possessions. He practised his philosophy and lived his life as a true Cynic, shamelessly rejecting societal norms and expectations. He begged for food, urinated and defecated wherever he pleased, ate whatever and wherever he liked and ridiculed people for their vanity and attachment to ideas and things that really don't matter. The word Cynic comes from the Greek kynikos, which means "dog-like"; Diogenes and his fellow Cynics were disparagingly called "dogs" because they lived like dogs on the street.

Cynicism was developed later by **Crates of Thebes** (*c*.365–*c*.285 BCE), a Greek philosopher who also gave away his fortune to live on the streets of Athens. He fell in love with and married **Hipparchia of Maronea** (*c*.350–*c*.280 BCE) – another Cynic and one of the first female philosophers. Theirs was a marriage and life of total equality, which was unheard of between a man and his wife in Ancient Athens. Crates wrote poems which advocated an ascetic (self-disciplined without any indulgences) life, untroubled by wants or desires. He believed the Cynic should be satisfied with what he has and encouraged people only to eat lentils because anything more luxurious could cause people to want more and become rebellious. Crates was teacher to Zeno of Citium, who developed Cynic ideas into the much more influential and far-reaching philosophy, Stoicism.

# STOICISM

As in Cynicism, virtue and living in accordance with nature and your natural state is at the heart of Stoicism. Stoic philosophers resonated with ordinary people, making it a popular and practical philosophy that people could actively apply in their lives. Initially founded in around 300 BCE by **Zeno of Citium** (*c.*334–*c.*262 BCE), an Ancient Greek philosopher and student of the Cynic philosopher, Crates of Thebes, Stoicism was further developed in the first century CE by the Roman philosophers Seneca (see page 75) and Epictetus (page 78) and the Roman emperor and philosopher Marcus Aurelius (page 81).

The main focus of Stoicism is on ethics, with the Stoics being heavily influenced by Socrates' ideas of the importance of "knowing thyself" through questioning one's beliefs and of living a life with high moral standards.

Central to Stoicism is the acknowledgement that most of what we experience is out of our control. What we *can* control is how we view what happens to us – by changing our perception of events, we can influence our emotional responses and thus avoid distressing feelings. Epictetus summed it up when he said: "Men are disturbed not by things but by their opinions about them."

Another answer to improve well-being, according to Stoicism, is to lower your expectations of life's events. Much disappointment and emotional suffering arises as a result of expecting things to turn out better than they actually do. Instead, Stoicism says that we should thank our lucky stars for what we do have and not be distraught by what we don't, and that it's pointless to worry about how things could have been otherwise. Life's too short.

Today, Stoic ideas are applied in Cognitive Behavioural Therapy (CBT). This approach to treating anxiety and depression encourages people to question and rationalize their interpretation of an event, just as Socrates advocated, which can in turn change their thoughts and beliefs about it. If we can use Stoic ideas to have more rational emotional responses, we can improve our mental health and well-being.

# SENECA
## c.4 BCE–65 CE

Seneca the Younger was born in Córdoba, Spain (then part of the Roman Empire) around 4 BCE and spent much of his life in Rome as a politician and writer (his tragic plays are said to have influenced Shakespeare). His letters and philosophical writings focused on ethics and were influenced by early Stoics such as Zeno.

He lived a very troubled life. He was often physically unwell and suffered terrible periods of depression. Around 41 CE he was exiled from Rome by the newly appointed Roman ruler, Claudius, for allegedly committing adultery with the sister of the previous emperor, Caligula, but he returned ten years later to tutor the soon-to-be Roman emperor, Nero. However, it would be Nero who would finally finish him off. Nero unjustly accused Seneca of plotting against him and ordered Seneca to commit suicide.

It was as a result of this hard and tumultuous life that Seneca focused on Stoic philosophy to ease his pain.

His writings, mostly in the form of letters, are a Stoic guide in dealing with life's adversities as well as life's good fortune.

And he did experience some good fortune – at one point he was one of the richest men in Rome – but he warned against wealth being misused or depended upon, saying, "the wise man regards wealth a slave, the fool a master".

He also warned against squandering the time you have. In his brief text, "On the Shortness of Life", he writes: "We are not given a short life but we make it short, and we are not ill-supplied but wasteful of it." He believed happiness lies in knowing yourself and having self-control, especially of the passions like anger and fear, and, like every good Stoic, he championed a bit of suffering as being character-building, saying, "suffering is a test that will strengthen an individual, while anger, grief and fear are emotional traps that will enslave them". In his *Letters to Lucilius*, which were written toward the end of his life, he contemplates death and the Stoic idea of confronting our fears, coming to terms with the worst of possibilities and courageously facing the inevitable, in life and death, in order to live life to the fullest.

When Seneca's life was cut short at Nero's behest, his death was horrific but "stoic". He calmly took some poison and slit his wrists, as was the tradition. Unfortunately, it is said that he bled very slowly and that the poison was also slow to act, so he took a hot bath in order to speed up the bleeding process – and ended up suffocating in the steam. Poor guy.

# EPICTETUS
## c.55–135 CE

Another influential Stoic, Epictetus, was born into slavery
in 55 CE and was treated mercilessly by his first owner,
suffering terrible injuries as a result of beatings. His
second owner, however, was much more humane: he took
Epictetus to Rome and allowed him to study under the Stoic
teacher, Musconius Rufus, and eventually gave Epictetus
his freedom, whereupon Epictetus turned to teaching.
No writings from Epictetus himself have survived, but his
student, Arrian, transcribed his teachings in the *Discourses
of Epictetus* and *Enchiridion (or Handbook) of Epictetus*.

Epictetus' Stoic teachings are very much intended for
ordinary people and draw upon his own experiences of
pain and suffering. He taught that even if our bodies are
enslaved, we all have free will over our minds – we can
control our beliefs and thoughts. Pretty much everything
else is outside our control, so it's not worth worrying
about. He believed unhappiness is a result of trying to

control what is not within your power, so understanding what you can and can't control is key. You are, however, in control of what you do, so you should choose your actions wisely.

Epictetus taught that we should never be troubled by loss because nothing actually belongs to us in the first place. He believed the only thing that is truly ours is our opinion, so taking responsibility for yourself and your opinions is key: you cannot blame anyone else for your misfortune because the misfortune itself is just an opinion – it is not misfortune that upsets us, but our judgement of it. Epictetus tells us that life will always throw up challenges and you will inevitably be hit by the odd curveball, but indulging in feelings of anger, outrage, frustration or unhappiness simply causes you more unnecessary pain. However, adopting a Stoic mindset of indifference or even optimism in the face of adversity will lead to true freedom and a state of *ataraxia* or peace of mind. Admiral James Stockdale, a US fighter pilot shot down during the Vietnam war, drew on his knowledge of Epictetus' teachings in order to endure seven-and-a-half years in captivity. He was savagely tortured, suffered horrific injuries and held in solitary confinement for years but managed to survive because of his heroic stoicism.

# MARCUS AURELIUS
## 121–180 CE

Marcus Aurelius was born in CE 121 and took an interest in philosophy early on in life. He was particularly interested in Epictetus' Stoic philosophy and turned to it throughout his life. He ruled the Roman Empire as emperor from CE 161 until his death in CE 180. His emperorship was riddled with difficulties – there were plagues, floods, earthquakes and uprisings to deal with – but, with Stoic wisdom to guide him, Marcus Aurelius governed brilliantly and is seen as the last of the "five good emperors".

He spent the last ten years of his life at war with Germanic tribes. It was during these challenging conflicts that Aurelius wrote *Meditations*, a Stoic guide to self-help. *Meditations* wasn't written for general consumption, he was journaling about his everyday experiences, writing down the things that were upsetting him and then analysing them, looking at them from different perspectives in order to find healthier attitudes toward his problems.

As a result, we have an idea of how one of the most powerful men in the world handled his fears and worries. His maxims and nuggets of self-help wisdom are transferable to the common man and have been inspirational to many, including US presidents such as George Washington and Bill Clinton, military leaders, and sports and business people. Even J. K. Rowling is a fan, tweeting that Marcus Aurelius never lets her down.

Like all good Stoics, Marcus Aurelius practised what he preached and really lived up to the Stoic principles of cultivating wisdom and virtue, behaving in a just way for the greater good, resisting temptation, and being indifferent to what was out of his control. He placed great importance on living mindfully, focusing on the job in hand and the present moment: "Remind yourself that past and future have no control over you. Only the present – and even that can be minimised. Just mark off its limits. And if your mind tries to claim that it can't, hold out against that."

Stoicism would continue to have a big influence on religious and philosophical thought for years to come.

# *Medieval and Renaissance Philosophy*

The Roman Empire reached its height in the second century CE and by the fourth century it was so huge it had been split into two – the East (Byzantine) and West – and Christianity had begun to replace pagan beliefs. Despite its power and influence, by the fifth century CE, the Empire was buckling under its own weight. The Western Empire became weak, and in 476 CE Rome was conquered and Europe fell into a state of turmoil, with barbarian tribes like the Goths, Huns, Vandals, Saxons and Vikings running amok, battling and invading. The Byzantine Empire continued for another thousand years, until it too succumbed to invading forces.

This period of world history between the fifth and fifteenth centuries – the Middle Ages or Medieval period – is sandwiched between the Ancient and the Modern. It is seen as a time of intellectual "bleurgh", with very little of note being accomplished. However, despite the tumultuous social and political conditions and the lack of historical records, philosophers carried on thinking. Philosophy in the West was dominated by the early Christian thinkers, and, from around the eleventh century, Scholasticism (the system of theology and philosophy taught in medieval universities, which emphasized Christian tradition and dogma – see also Thomas Aquinas, page 87) became the dominant method of critical thought.

Meanwhile in the East, a new religion, Islam, was gaining traction. The prophet Muhammad preached a new faith based on the Qu'ran, scriptures that he believed had been revealed to him by God through the angel Jibrīl over a period of 23 years from 609 CE. What followed was a period of Islamic expansion and a "Golden Age" of Islamic thought. Cities such as Cairo and Córdoba in the new Islamic empires became hubs of intellectual activity, and philosophers flourished.

Crucial to the world of philosophy was the translation of many of Aristotle's works into Arabic. Muslim philosophers such as **Ibn Sina**, or "Avicenna" in Latin (980–1037), and **Ibn Rushd**, or "Averroes" (1126–1198), studied the works of Aristotle and Plato alongside Islamic doctrine and attempted to come up with logical reasons for the existence of God. Ibn Sina, a pre-eminent physician and philosopher, in his philosophical work *The Book of Healing*, takes one of Aristotle's arguments – the distinction between necessary and possible existence – and takes it to its logical conclusion. It's only possible for things to exist because of the existence of a thing prior to it. We can track back existence to a first cause; something that exists independently of anything else. And, for Ibn Sina, that was God, the Necessary Existent.

With works by Aristotle and Plato having been translated from Ancient Greek into Arabic, they were then translated into Hebrew and Latin and rediscovered in the West, and so Christian philosophers set about trying to reconcile the philosophies of Aristotle (who didn't believe in a personal god, creation, or an immortal soul as the Scholastics would have it) and Plato with Christian faith. The Jewish philosopher and physician, **Maimonides**, who was born in 1135 in Córdoba, stated in his *Guide for the Perplexed* that any contradiction between reason and the word of God is down to the reader's interpretation of the Torah, and so they must go back and read again.

Reason, he believed, is able to confirm the truth of religion. Maimonides' attempts to reconcile Aristotle's empiricist ideas with scripture influenced the Christian philosophers of the West and, in particular, Thomas Aquinas.

# THOMAS AQUINAS
## 1225–1274

Thomas Aquinas was born in 1225 into Italian nobility, and was a philosopher and theologian in the Scholastic tradition – from the Latin *scholasticus* meaning school, referring to the style of teaching and learning that took place in monastic schools and medieval universities. The Scholastic method consists of "disputations" or formalized debates designed to get to the truth through logical argument and the elimination of contradictions. The Scholastics studied the texts of the Ancient Greeks, translated the Arabic commentaries of the Islamic philosophers, and tried to harmonize philosophy and their Christian faith.

Aquinas tried to do just that and wrote disputations on all sorts of theological and philosophical themes. His most famous work, *Summa Theologica*, sets out his Christian philosophy. Like Aristotle, he believed truth is known through natural discovery and reason, but Aquinas believed some truths were knowable through divine revelation. He distinguished between the two but saw them as complementing each other. In *Summa*, he attempted to prove the existence of God through five "ways".

Aquinas accepted that the universe and all things within it constantly move with whatever is changing, having been changed by something else, but he thought that an unchanging thing must start this chain of motion. So, his first point in his five ways to prove the existence of God was that there was a "first mover" and that was God – God is the "unmoved mover" from whom all movement and change proceeds.

His second point, and at the heart of his theory, was his belief that God is the First Cause, or the thing that caused the universe. The First Cause argument tells us that everything is caused by something and that you can trace the origins of everything back to an original, first cause. Aquinas argued that logically something must have started the chain of causation; the cosmos had to start somewhere (obviously the theory of the Big Bang had not been explored at that point in history) and, in keeping with his religious beliefs, he said the uncaused cause was God. This seemed at odds with Aristotle's belief that the universe had always existed. For Aristotle, the universe had been and is always moving and changing so there couldn't have been a first cause or uncaused creation – the cosmos is just an infinite chain of causation.

The third point was that God is the Necessary Being, the non-contingent (God is not contingent on any other being, unlike everything else). The fourth point in the system was God's place as the pinnacle of perfection against which all things are compared on a scale of degrees. And, lastly, the fifth point was that God is the highest intelligence, who directs nature to act toward end goals. Of course, there were many flaws in Aquinas' reasoning, but he had a huge influence on Christian teaching during the Middle Ages and is considered a saint and one of the greatest theologians by the Catholic Church.

# WILLIAM OF OCKHAM
## c.1287–c.1347

Another controversial theologian and philosopher, who was excommunicated for his ideas, William of Ockham, went a step further than Aquinas with philosophical reasoning, by asserting that the existence of God could never actually be proven rationally. He distinguished between philosophical reasoning and divine revelation or faith and didn't see a link between the two.

William of Ockham was all about keeping things simple. His law of parsimony – known as Ockham's (or Occam's, from the Latin) razor – had a significant influence on philosophy and scientific practice. "Parsimony" means to be frugal with resources, and Ockham argued that any theory should explain a phenomenon using the simplest possible ("most frugal") explanation. So, if you are presented with multiple explanations for something, you should always opt for the one that depends upon the fewest assumptions (variables, factors or causes) or the simplest, most logical explanation. For instance, I see water dripping through the ceiling from the bathroom above. Possible explanations are: (a) the bath is leaking and water is seeping through the ceiling; or (b) someone has left the plug in the bath with the tap running, and water has flooded the bathroom. Out of the two explanations (a) is most likely because it's the simplest with the fewest variables; (b) requires someone else to be involved along with a plug left in the bath, a tap left running, and a flood! Occam's razor tells us to choose the most straightforward scenario in any given situation and, chances are, you will be right most of the time.

# THE RENAISSANCE

By the fourteenth century a renaissance or "rebirth" of artistic and intellectual activity was underway. Emanating from Italy, with "Renaissance men" such as Leonardo da Vinci and Michelangelo embodying the term, and making dramatic advances in painting, sculpture, engineering, architecture, physics, music and philosophy, this cultural movement influenced the arts, science, politics, religion and philosophy. Thinkers turned their attention to the more human aspects of philosophy, focusing very much on the reality of the human experience in the here and now. Renaissance humanists were thinkers of the fourteenth to the sixteenth centuries who liberated learning from stuffy Scholasticism and focused on the humanities, studying history, poetry and philosophy, so that people could engage in and make a difference to their communities. The Renaissance humanists rediscovered the literature of Ancient Greece, along with the works of Plato and schools of thought such as Stoicism and Epicureanism. Theology and philosophy became more and more detached from one another, with philosophy beginning to gain greater autonomy. Radical thinkers, such as **Desiderius Erasmus** (1466–1536) and **Martin Luther** (1483–1546), embraced a more critical and reasoned approach to the Catholic Church, questioning the morality of the Catholic Church's leaders and their teachings.

It was Johannes Gutenberg's movable-type printing press that truly revolutionized the world in the mid-fifteenth century, enabling books to be produced much more quickly and cheaply than before: this had a far-reaching and profound impact on learning and the spread of ideas to all members of society – not just learned theologians and lofty philosophers.

# NICCOLÒ MACHIAVELLI
## 1469–1527

The Renaissance humanists turned their gaze toward the humanities and wanted to explore real-life experiences. And there was no one more steeped in the reality of human behaviour than the Political philosopher and Florentine diplomat Niccolò Machiavelli. Machiavelli took his experiences and observations of the murky world of Florentine politics and, in 1513, published a sort of "manual for leaders" called *The Prince*, in which he advocated dispensing with just and virtuous acts of leadership such as those of Marcus Aurelius in favour of a much more cut-throat and cunning approach – one we would now call "Machiavellian". He coached leaders in how to gain power, and, more importantly, in how to maintain it. He suggested that people are, generally, pretty evil – "of mankind we may say in general they are fickle, hypocritical and greedy of gain" – so leaders need to be ruthless and rule by striking fear into their subjects. A prince should be willing to do whatever it takes to reach his goals, even if that means acting cruelly.

Machiavelli challenged the idealism of politics, insisting that rulers govern according to the reality of the social and political stage rather than the ideal. This move toward realism was also impacting natural philosophy, and great thinkers like Francis Bacon were beginning to make revolutionary discoveries in the field of science.

# FRANCIS BACON
## 1561–1626

Sir Francis Bacon, an English philosopher, statesman, essayist and scientist, was born into an extremely well-connected family in 1561. He studied and practised law and was a successful politician, securing many prestigious government appointments, including Lord High Chancellor in 1618. His life was colourful: he was terrible with money, lived a lavish lifestyle and, in 1598, was even arrested for his bad debts. He fell into further disrepute in 1621 when he was charged with corruption and bribery, had a brief stay in the Tower of London, and was banned from taking political office.

Despite all these shenanigans, he wrote some influential works and developed "the scientific method" – a way of acquiring knowledge through observation, experiment and deduction. His insistence that truth required robust empirical evidence usurped the previously established methodology, which was based on the premise that scientific truth could be reached by way of authoritative argument alone, and brought science much closer to what we know today. *A priori* knowledge, or knowledge that is independent of experience, was out and *a posteriori* knowledge, or knowledge that depends on experience or empirical evidence, was in. He saw advances in scientific knowledge as essential to improving people's lives, rather than being about academic or personal prowess, and stood by the aphorism "knowledge is power".

# Modern Philosophy

With its artistic and cultural advancements, the Renaissance period (around 1400 to 1600) marks the start of the Modern era in history and philosophy. Thinkers were courageously challenging the dominant beliefs of the Catholic Church, which had been all-powerful throughout Europe. In 1632 Galileo Galilei, the pre-eminent scientist, published *Dialogue Concerning the Two Chief World Systems*, which called into question the Church's Ptolemaic view of the universe: that the Earth is the centre of the universe and the Sun revolves around it. Galileo used the newly invented telescope and backed up the Copernican view that actually the Earth and all other planets orbited the Sun. The Catholic Church didn't like this idea and, after a trial by the inquisition, Galileo was found guilty of heresy and put under house arrest for the rest of his life. And his book was banned.

Galileo was an Empiricist – he used his observations and experiences of the world to come up with new ideas. And it was the Empiricists, with their insistence that all knowledge originates in sensory experience, who formed part of the Modern philosophical landscape. Philosophers such as John Locke and David Hume took this empirical approach, embodying this Age of Enlightenment.

On the other hand, there was a group of Modern philosophers who based their theses on Rationalism – the principle that knowledge originates in the mind and some truths can be known through reasoning alone. Philosophers such as René Descartes (page 103), Baruch Spinoza and Gottfried Wilhelm Leibniz used their mathematical knowledge and reasoning and applied them to all learning, using Continental Rationalism to advance philosophical ideas into the Modern Age.

In addition to these two distinct practices of philosophy, Empiricism and Rationalism, there were huge developments in Political philosophy, with thinkers such as Thomas Hobbes (page 114), Jean-Jacques Rousseau (page 121) and Immanuel Kant (page 129) contributing revolutionary ideas.

Modern philosophers were beginning to unshackle themselves from the chains of theology and the antiquated theories of the Ancients that had kept philosophical thought tightly contained. As the Modern period progressed, the Church's grip on society weakened and thinking became less restricted – unorthodox beliefs began to be more freely discussed than before. In the words of Immanuel Kant, in order to become enlightened, people needed to "dare to know!"

# RATIONALISM

Rationalism is the understanding that truths and knowledge are reached through reasoning rather than relying on religious beliefs, emotional responses or sensory experiences. We can work things out by using what we know already and come to a conclusion logically, like the Scholastics deducing that God exists, or **Albert Einstein** (1879–1955) taking pre-existing scientific knowledge and rationally, or mathematically, working out new theories.

Einstein was a great believer in intuition playing a part in discovery. Working alongside deduction and logical reasoning, intuition can provide the scientist, philosopher or mathematician with a "hunch" to start their investigation.

Some Rationalists argue that we possess innate ideas, that knowledge that is part of our nature. This harks back to Plato's Theory of Forms and the idea that we are all born with a certain amount of knowledge within us, and that learning is simply accessing that understanding. So much of what we know is *a priori* knowledge – it is based on something we know already.

# RENÉ DESCARTES
## 1596–1650

René Descartes of "I think, therefore I am" fame is considered the father of Modern philosophy and one of the first Rationalist philosophers. Born in 1596 and educated in the Scholastic tradition in France, he studied law but opted to join the Dutch army rather than pursue a legal career. After many years of army postings and thoughtful wanderings, mixing with all kinds of people and experiencing life's rich offerings, he settled in Holland where he set about writing his treatises and modernizing the worlds of mathematics, science and philosophy.

In 1637 he wrote *Discourse on Method* followed, in 1641, by *Meditations on First Philosophy*, in which he sought to create a philosophy that was distinct from those that had come before. His method was based on careful reasoning. He was a Rationalist advocating a slow, steady, robust investigation of all knowledge in order to eliminate uncertainty. For Descartes, everything was open to dispute. His philosophical and epistemological quest was for universal answers – he wanted to believe only in knowledge that was beyond all doubt. This proved incredibly difficult because he knew that all his knowledge had come to him through his senses – and that his senses could be deceived.

He asked questions such as: What if life is a dream? And, What if a devil has merely created our perception of what we are experiencing and of everything we know? Through a process of stringent reasoning, he concluded that everything he thought he knew was open to doubt except for one thing: the fact that he was thinking about it all in the first place. Descartes had discovered the one fundamental, basic truth – "I think, therefore I am." The only thing we know with certainty is that we exist; we can doubt our bodies and all other material things, but the fact that we are thinking means our minds exist.

This idea led to his examination of the mind and body as two different kinds of substance, an idea known as Cartesian dualism. Like Plato and Aristotle 2,000 years before, he believed the mind, or soul, to be separate from the body. He reasoned you could take the body apart but not the mind, so, although linked, they must be different.

Using Descartes' methods, human beings could reason their way to truth. *Cogito, ergo sum* is the most famous philosophical quote of all time, and it catapulted philosophy into the Modern Age.

# EMPIRICISM

If Rationalism is the acquiring of knowledge through reasoning with nothing needed but your mind and intellect, Empiricism is the opposite. It is knowledge gained through sensory experience, through experimentation and through experiencing the world – it's *a posteriori* knowledge. Empiricists traditionally reject the idea that all human beings are born with innate ideas. Instead they believe our minds are a *tabula rasa* or a blank slate, and that our experiences inform our knowledge.

Empiricism goes back to Aristotle and his method of understanding the world through observation. Aristotle represents the Empiricists, while Plato's ideas about innate knowledge and Metaphysics are Rationalist. In Raphael's famous Renaissance painting, *The School of Athens* (*c.*1510), a fresco situated in the Vatican, we see Plato and Aristotle taking centre stage: Plato, the Rationalist, points up to the heavens and his World of Forms, while Aristotle gestures toward the floor, his Empirical ideas firmly grounded in experience.

# JOHN LOCKE
## 1632–1704

The idea that human beings start life as a blank slate
(or *tabula rasa*) and all knowledge is based on sensory
experience gained throughout life was proposed by the
English philosopher, John Locke, in his major philosophical
work *An Essay Concerning Human Understanding*,
published in 1690. According to Locke, knowledge is made
up of ideas: we start with a sensory idea and then reflect
upon it; we think about it, doubt it, reason about it, and
create more ideas. The ideas can be simple or complex.
Simple ideas are single experiences – the red of an apple.
Complex ideas are a number of simple ideas combined –
the combination of red, sweet and firm gives us the *idea*
of an apple. Complex ideas can also develop in the mind
through reflection, so we can know all about apples by
considering the look, feel, taste, where they grow, and so on.

Locke tells us that our understanding of everything
is limited, that it is a result of our experiences and the

ideas we have developed in our thinking minds. This was a challenge to the Rationalists' theory about innate ideas (that we can gain knowledge of something without having to experience it). For instance, Locke said there is no empirical evidence to back up Plato's claim that we are born with a universal, innate knowledge and only have to access that knowledge; as far as Locke was concerned there was zero empirical evidence that babies are born with knowledge, and the idea that innate ideas exist beyond human existence is ridiculous because all ideas are only possible in the human mind.

John Locke was also well known for his Political philosophy. He had a great influence on the development of Liberalism during the seventeenth century, which we will look at later (see page 117).

But for now, it is safe to say, as one of the first of the British Empiricists, Locke and his theories of Epistemology made a big impact, influencing George Berkeley and David Hume, both of whom were highly sceptical about whether anything existed beyond the mind.

# DAVID HUME
## 1711–1776

David Hume was a Scottish philosopher during the Age of Enlightenment. He was an Empiricist, an agnostic bordering on an atheist and a Sceptic. He took John Locke's empirical approach and attempted a scientific study of human nature. One of the great Modern philosophers, he influenced Immanuel Kant and Arthur Schopenhauer, was appreciated by Voltaire, and was a friend of Jean-Jacques Rousseau (although they later had a big falling out).

In his great work, *A Treatise of Human Nature*, published in 1739, Hume set out to create a "science of man", looking for universal laws of human nature. He wanted to discover why humans believe what they do. As an ardent Empiricist, he asserted that all knowledge and ideas are a product of sensory experience that is perceived by the mind, and that you cannot prove that anything exists beyond the mind. For Hume, human beliefs exist within the mind as either impressions (sensations, passions and emotions) or ideas (thinking, imagining and reasoning about the impressions). He distinguished between two categories of human knowledge: matters of fact (ideas based on experience or observation), and "relations of ideas" (thinking about the relationship and associations between ideas). Hume deduced that the idea of God is nonsensical because it is not based on sensory data – you cannot prove the existence of God through experience or reasoning, it's just a belief that some people have. So, to try to convince others that God really does exist is pointless. This was very controversial during the eighteenth century when people, scientists included, were saying that God is the Divine Architect of all things, an all-knowing being.

Hume also argued that custom and habit play a large role in the conclusions we come to about things in the world. What he's saying is that a lot of our knowledge is based on previous examples or experiences, such as "the sun will rise tomorrow" – there isn't any solid proof to say the sun actually will rise again tomorrow beyond actually experiencing it tomorrow (which we can't do because it's in the future). So, we are making an assumption that it will rise tomorrow: we can't rationally prove it, but we believe that it will. For Hume, a lot of what we know and believe about the world is not based on rational thinking, it is based on what we feel to be true: what has happened in the past together with common sense. The sun will almost definitely rise tomorrow because it always has done. And that is fine, because that belief works for us, we don't have to rationally prove it beyond all doubt like Descartes tried to – for Hume that is just a waste of time. Hume was therefore a Sceptic, but he was also all about common sense: many of the beliefs we have are impossible to prove 100 per cent, but they work well for us and that is perfectly fine.

# Political Philosophy

Political philosophy is concerned with questions about the state and government. It delves into issues of politics, freedom, justice and laws. It considers the individual within a society and the individual's rights to life, liberty, property, the pursuit of happiness and free speech. As part of Ethics, Political philosophers ask how society should be set up and how we should expect individuals to behave within that society in order to maximize the benefits for the greatest number. Political philosophy is a world of -isms: liberalism, capitalism, socialism, Marxism, libertarianism, conservatism, anarchism, nationalism, fascism, totalitarianism, feminism, egalitarianism...

A major turning point in Western Political philosophy came about during the Age of Reason, from the late seventeenth and into the eighteenth century. Thomas Hobbes got the Modern (Political) philosophical ball rolling with his harsh theory of the natural state of human beings, and John Locke's liberal ideas were immortalized in the American Declaration of Independence which then impacted on the French Revolution via the French Enlightenment philosophers Voltaire and Jean-Jacques Rousseau.

# THOMAS HOBBES
## 1588–1679

Thomas Hobbes was an English philosopher and a foundational figure in Modern Political philosophy. He studied at Oxford, but disliked the scholastic methods and, influenced by the scientific thought of Galileo and Francis Bacon, favoured a more empiricist approach. His major work *Leviathan* (published 1651) was written during the English Civil Wars, which found the Roundheads (Parliamentarians) fighting the Cavaliers (Royalists) for control. Hobbes was a Royalist who believed monarchs made the best rulers. This made him unpopular with the Parliamentarians, who had flung Charles I in prison and gained control, so Hobbes fled to Paris and, for a short time, tutored the Prince of Wales, future King Charles II.

In *Leviathan*, he laid out his theory of the relationship between the individual and society, which became known as "social contract theory". Hobbes took a very mechanistic view of human beings, seeing them as machines that are in constant motion driven by forces outside of themselves. He believed that people are in a constant state of attraction and repulsion, protecting themselves and trying to attract things that are good or repelling things that are bad. They are inherently selfish and greedy and will do whatever they can to protect themselves, get as much material wealth as they can, and fight for power.

In Hobbes' vision, this fundamental flaw could lead to war and destruction and, if left ungoverned, individuals would descend into what he called a "state of nature" and a "war of all against all". In order to avoid harsh conflict and the possibility of death, in his doctrine, individuals can give up their natural right to absolute liberty in exchange for protection by a sovereign ruler. The sovereign state would have absolute power, and be known as the great Leviathan.

John Locke (see page 108) developed Hobbes' social contract idea and, in his *Second Treatise of Government* (1689), suggested that any ruler's power should be conditional: if the ruler fails to live up to their subjects' expectations, the people have a right to appoint another ruler. He rejected Hobbes' idea of an absolute ruler and believed true sovereignty lay in the hands of the people. He advocated a constitutional monarchy with executive power and a periodically elected parliament having legislative power. His ideas about the rights of the individual, the natural equality of men, and the importance of rulers to be representative and consented to by the people, form the basis of Liberalism.

# LIBERALISM

Liberalism has its origins in the Renaissance period (fourteenth to seventeenth centuries), when thinkers began to question the authority of the Church. The word "liberal" comes from the Latin word *liber* meaning "free" or "not a slave". It was during the eighteenth century and the Age of Enlightenment that Liberalism became a recognizable movement, greatly influencing the War of Independence (1775-1783) in America and the French Revolution (1789-1799). In England, the Liberal movement began in 1689 with the publication of John Locke's *Two Treatises of Government*, which outlined his "natural rights" theory - that every individual has a right to life, liberty and property.

In Liberalism, individuals' rights should be protected by a government, which should be limited, democratically elected, and representative of all individuals in society. Government is only justified if it maximizes the freedom of the individuals and protects the individuals from any invasions of rights – an idea that originated in Hobbes' "social contract" (which was later expanded upon by Locke). Central to Liberalism is individual liberty, freedom of thought, freedom of speech and freedom to own property. Religious tolerance and civil rights including women's rights and racial equality are also key to Liberal thought.

# VOLTAIRE
## 1694–1778

Voltaire, real name François-Marie Arouet, was born in Paris in 1694. He was a philosopher, poet, playwright, novelist and essayist, whose outspoken writings and critiques of the French government led to him spending 11 months imprisoned in the Bastille and, in 1726, being exiled to England. During his time in England, he read about John Locke's concepts of civil liberties, and was also inspired by the empiricist science of Isaac Newton with his explanations of nature, based on rational principles. He embraced these ideas and set about challenging the Church and its *irrational*, superstitious doctrines that were being used to maintain power and control in his own country. In *Philosophical Letters on the English Nation*, published in 1734, he celebrated the liberal ideas of Locke and condemned French society, which was based on its absolute monarchy, aristocracy and religious intolerance, very much influencing the revolutionaries, who succeeded in overthrowing the French monarchy 11 years after Voltaire died.

A true Enlightenment philosopher, he always questioned the world and how people lived in it, even going as far as declaring that certainty is absurd. Voltaire admits doubt is an uncomfortable condition, but, for him, it is a more logical stance to take given that most theories and facts have been reworked at some point and can be challenged at any time: facts and truths are just works in progress. Voltaire could see that putting blind faith in authoritative statements was easier than challenging them or thinking for yourself, but this latter was essential.

He was a believer in liberty, religious tolerance and in challenging injustice, and was a critic of French colonialism. He wrote a history of the Middle Ages that didn't just focus on the Scholasticism of Europe but explored the influences of Arabic thinking and ideas emanating from China and Japan. He fought for freedom of expression and free speech and, although not a direct quote from Voltaire, the Voltairean principle that "I disapprove of what you say, but I will defend to the death your right to say it" is at the core of Liberal ideas of free speech.

# JEAN-JACQUES ROUSSEAU
## 1712–1778

Jean-Jacques Rousseau was born in Geneva in 1712, and his early life was a mix of tragic luck and fortuitous encounters. His mother died shortly after childbirth and his childhood was unsettled, with very limited formal education. He spent periods wandering as a vagabond, experiencing the goodwill of those often less well off than himself and, as a result, always had respect for the underdog. His luck changed during his twenties, when he lived with a noblewoman who possessed a vast library, and it was during these years that he dedicated himself to studying philosophy, mathematics and music. He moved to Paris in 1742 and came into contact with Voltaire, whose intellect he greatly admired, though they had different approaches to their thinking.

Seen as the father of the Romantic movement, Rousseau was inspired by feeling and "sensibility" rather than reason. He didn't see any need to prove God's existence through reasoning like the Medieval philosophers did, as he thought God was revealed to each person individually. God's presence would be felt in the heart, in the goodness of the soul, and in the awe and wonder of the natural world.

Rousseau's most influential work, *The Social Contract* (1762), sets out his Political philosophy. He explores the nature of man and, in contrast with the Hobbesian idea of the human "state of nature" being fundamentally malevolent, Rousseau argues human beings are naturally peaceful and good with innate compassion and empathy.

It is only through the process of civilization that man becomes bad. This social civilization occurred because of the emergence of private ownership of property, which created inequality and conflict and natural freedoms were lost:

> *Man is born free; and everywhere he is in chains. Those who think themselves masters over others are indeed greater slaves than they.*

The social contracts that people have entered into in modern societies have compounded inequality, and so

Rousseau suggests an alternative to Hobbes' contract. In Rousseau's city-state, *people* would have sovereignty and make laws based on the collective "general will". People would give up individual freedoms for a collective or civil freedom that would work in the interests of all and diminish inequality. Rousseau's theory was adopted by the French revolutionaries, who took his words, "man is born free; and everywhere he is in chains", as one of their rallying cries. Some critics argued his views were troubling, as they favoured the liberty of the group over the freedom of the individual, but his politically enlightened ideas offered a viable and radical alternative to the injustices experienced by a society ruled by a wealthy minority. Around a hundred years later it was Rousseau's critique of capitalist society that influenced Karl Marx's revolutionary ideas, as he urged the proletariat (workers) to rise up and fight for equality and freedom for, as Marx would echo Rousseau in his *Communist Manifesto*, they have "nothing to lose but their chains".

# JOHN STUART MILL
## 1806–1873

John Stuart Mill was born in London in 1806 to James Mill, a philosopher and historian who had high hopes for his son. With advice from the Utilitarian philosopher, Jeremy Bentham, James set out to educate his son rigorously in preparation for a life of continuing the Utilitarian cause. Utilitarianism is a movement in Ethics that asserts that any action is right so long as it maximizes happiness – "the greatest good for the greatest number" is its maxim.

After having a mental breakdown at the age of 20 as a result of his stressful and demanding childhood, John Stuart Mill took comfort in the Romantic poets, and also in the Positivism of Auguste Comte. Positivism states that the only authentic knowledge is scientific knowledge, and it influenced Mill's *A System of Logic* (1843), where he set out to apply the scientific method to social, as well as natural, phenomena. In his popular *Principles of Political Economy* (1848), Mill advocated free market economies, whereby supply and demand dictate the price of goods and there is little, if any, government interference, even though Mill was actually a promoter of worker cooperatives that give workers a stake in businesses rather than all the power and profits going to the capitalist owners.

His most famous and influential work is *On Liberty*, which was published in 1859. Here he explores ideas regarding the freedom of the individual within society. His "harm principle" sets out his idea that the only legitimate use of coercion in a society would be in self-defence or in order to defend others from harm. Other than that, people should be free to do whatever they like to themselves, as long as it doesn't impinge on another's freedom or harm them. Mill passionately defended freedom of speech, seeing it as imperative for social and intellectual development and progress.

His liberal views influenced socialism, libertarianism and feminism. In his 1869 essay, *The Subjection of Women*, which was written with inspiration and ideas from his wife, Harriett Taylor Mill, he argued for female emancipation, changes in the marriage laws, and equality of opportunity and education between the sexes, which would not just benefit the individual but society as a whole – very Utilitarian. He was an energetic political and social reformer and an advocate for workers' rights; he campaigned for the abolition of slavery; and, when he became the Liberal Member of Parliament for Westminster, he was the first person to call for universal suffrage. He strove to improve British society wherever possible and was one of Britain's greatest Modern philosophers.

# IDEALISM

Idealism says that reality, or existence, is all in the mind. For Idealists, it is ideas or thoughts that create reality, so Metaphysical explanations start from this point of view. René Descartes was one of the first philosophers to build his theories from this Idealist stance when he argued that the fundamental nature of reality is in our consciousness, that the reality of the external world of objects can be doubted and is merely perceived by the mind. Idealism, therefore, is the opposite of Materialism, which says that matter is the fundamental substance and everything, even consciousness and the mind, comes from material interactions.

Philosophers divide Idealism broadly into two camps: *Subjective* and *Objective* Idealism. Subjective

Idealists take into account what we experience and sense in the here and now, but ultimately believe that reality is simply perceived by the mind. George Berkeley, the eighteenth-century Irish philosopher, called it Immaterialism, saying the material world doesn't exist, and summed it up with the Latin phrase *"esse est percepi"*, or "to be is to be perceived".

Objective Idealism goes a step further than Subjective Idealism (which says that reality exists in the individual mind), and argues that an objective consciousness exists beyond and independently from human mental activity.

Immanuel Kant pondered the reality of existence for years, and eventually came up with his own idealism – Transcendental Idealism.

# IMMANUEL KANT
## 1724–1804

Immanuel Kant is considered one of the most important philosophers of Modern Western thought, and he sowed the seeds for the German Idealism of the nineteenth century. His works cover Epistemology, Metaphysics and Ethics, and his most groundbreaking work deals with philosophy of the mind. *The Critique of Pure Reason* (1781) was ten years in the making. Through careful and critical reasoning, Kant set out to bring together the two camps of Epistemology – Rationalism (see page 101) and Empiricism (see page 106).

He distinguishes between analytic propositions and synthetic propositions. Analytic propositions are things that are true because of what they literally mean, for example "all women are female". This is a truth of reason, we don't need proof that all women are female because we know the definition of women is that they are female. Synthetic propositions bring in another element, one that is experiential or requires observation, for example "all women are gentle". The gentle bit does not define all women but possibly some women, and you would need to investigate this statement to declare it true.

As well as distinguishing between these two types of truth, he also considers how truths are known, whether *a priori* (knowledge that comes from reasoning without any need for experience – for example, analytic propositions), or *a posteriori* (knowledge that comes from experience). (See page 41.) He argued that our knowledge of the world can be a combination of the two: the mind experiences the objects and, through reasoning, is able to conceive of them.

Kant asserts that we are all seeing the world through a filter, which is the mind. It is the mind that creates the experiences, processes the sensory information, and creates objects situated in space and time – this is part of our intuitive experience and perception of the world. The human mind creates the world rather than the world being etched on the human mind. This is the *phenomenal* world – it is the world we perceive. Kant argues that knowing what objects are like beyond their appearance or "in and of themselves" is impossible for us to grasp. He argues that everything in the universe exists on a much deeper level, which Kant calls the *noumenal* world, but we just don't have the sensory or intellectual capacity to understand it. This is where the "transcendental" part comes in: to objectively know an object we would have to transcend the limitations of our understanding and perceptions.

He explained his theory, called the "Categorical Imperative", in his 1785 work, *Groundwork for the Metaphysics of Morals,* where he suggests that we should always behave in ways that we would want to become a universal law. In a nutshell, you are responsible for your own actions and whatever *you* do, expect others to do too – much like the Golden Rule we discussed on page 61.

# MARY WOLLSTONECRAFT
## 1759–1797

Finally, a woman! A female philosopher! Apart from Hipparchia of Maronea (who was married to the Cynic, Crates of Thebes, with whom she had a union based on total equality), who got a mention way back in the Ancient philosophy section on Cynicism, and who was one of the first female philosophers, the field of Western philosophy has been largely dominated by men.

Mary Wollstonecraft, born in 1759, was a writer and philosopher, and was considered one of the first feminist philosophers, inspiring the feminist movement of the late nineteenth century. She lived an exciting and unconventional life, particularly for a woman in the eighteenth century. She opened a school in Newington Green, got caught up in the French Revolution (she wrote historical accounts about it, advocating republicanism and condemning monarchy and hereditary privilege), and had a relationship with an American adventurer with whom she had a child out of wedlock. She later married the Anarchist philosopher, William Godwin, with whom she had a second daughter, Mary Wollstonecraft Godwin. Tragically Mary died 11 days after giving birth to her daughter, at the age of 38. She lived a short but remarkable life. (Mary's second daughter, Mary Wollstonecraft Godwin, went on to marry the Romantic poet Percy Bysshe Shelley and became Mary Shelley, author of *Frankenstein*.)

*A Vindication of the Rights of Women*, which was published in 1792, is her best-known work. Here she presented women as vital to the country as educators of children and argued for equal rights for women, including a right to education – just like their male counterparts. She vociferously disputed Jean-Jacques Rousseau's assertion in his book *Émile* that women should only be educated for the pleasure of men, if at all. Wollstonecraft argued that men denying education to women had turned women into "toys" for men. She rejected the view of women as objects to be admired or property to be traded in marriage, believing that if you give girls an education and develop their minds, they will grow into "companions" for their husbands as opposed to mere wives. She urged women to think rationally and not be slaves to sensibility. With reason and feeling working in tandem, each informing the other, women can be of utmost value and will help "refine civilization". Mary Wollstonecraft set the ball rolling for feminist philosophers. With her radical, independent approach to life and learning, alongside her literary accomplishments, she was a true trailblazer and remains a feminist role model for women to this day.

# KARL MARX
## 1818–1883

Karl Marx was a German philosopher and political and economic theorist whose philosophy was influenced by Immanuel Kant, Georg Hegel and French social theorists such as Jean-Jacques Rousseau. He spent time in Paris, where he established a lifelong friendship and intellectual partnership with Friedrich Engels, learned about the plight of the working classes in nineteenth-century England and became a communist. In 1849, after years of moving around Europe, being ousted from one country or another because of his radical political views, he moved to London, where he remained for the rest of his life. His life was fraught with ill health and poverty and only three of his seven children survived, but, even so, he went on to become the most influential philosopher and political theorist the world has ever known.

He set out his theory of history, or "historical materialism", in *The German Ideology* (written *c.*1845, though not published until 1932). In it he developed a view of history based on "dialectical materialism", a concept influenced by Hegel's dialectic (which says that everything is in a continual state of change with opposites interacting and reacting). An idea, or *thesis*, reacts to its *antithesis* and the resulting tension gives rise to a resolution, or new idea, in the form of a *synthesis*, and this process is continually causing ideas to change and develop. Hegel was applying this concept to the mental world of ideas and spiritual development, but Marx applied Hegel's dialectic to the material world and the world of production and economy. He was analysing how societies have organized themselves in relation to the material world and studying how people create and produce things to live. He found that it was the struggle, or *tension*, between classes – slaves versus owners, workers versus capitalists – that brought about changes in the mode of production (how things are produced, with what resources, who produces them and the relations between people who own and govern the land/factories/industries and the workers), and thus societal and historical changes.

The year 1848 saw the publication of *The Communist Manifesto* by Marx and Engels, where they defined communism using dialectical materialism and class struggle as a basis for their ideology.

After settling in London in 1849, Marx continued this work, spending his days writing in the reading room of the British Museum, to produce his most famous work *Capital* (*Das Kapital*, 1867). *Capital* is a political and economic analysis of the development of capitalism that delved more deeply into the themes set out in the *Manifesto*. Focusing on economics he explained in detail how capitalism exploited the majority of people for the benefit of the few, how it was ultimately unstable because it cannot endlessly provide profits, and how capitalism would inevitably fall as a result of the masses becoming conscious of their alienation and exploitation and enacting a revolution that reorganized society into one based on a fairer, egalitarian economic system – communism.

Marx died in London in 1883, just 15 months after his wife, to whom he was devoted. He was buried in the family tomb, in Highgate Cemetery, which bears his words, "The philosophers have only interpreted the world in various ways – the point however is to change it" as well as the last line of *The Communist Manifesto*, "Workers of All Lands Unite". Marx believed his philosophy should actively change the world, and boy was he right!

# MARXISM

Marxism is the philosophical, political and social doctrine based on the ideas of Karl Marx and Friedrich Engels. It underpins communism and starts with Marx's ideas about dialectical materialism, which suggests that it is predominantly the tensions between classes with opposing interests that has driven historical change. Historically, human beings have organized themselves cooperatively around producing the things required to live. It's only when a surplus is created, profits are to be had, and private property comes into the mix, that inequality and discord arise. Divisions of labour occur and individuals lose control of their productive situation.

Marx believed human beings gain their humanity through their work, and that nineteenth-century industrialization and capitalist societies were exploiting and alienating people. The *proletariat*, or workers, no longer had any control over their work and were increasingly alienated from the means of production (the factories, machinery and materials, as well as how the labour force was organized), which was owned by the *bourgeoisie*. Marx predicted that the workers would get so fed up with the exhausting and exploitative conditions in which they were forced to work that they would rise up and take control of the means of production, transferring ownership from the bourgeoisie to the proletariat. This collective ownership of production would reconnect people with their humanity, because the proletariat would have regained control over their own labour.

This new "Communist" society would be classless and based on cooperation and equality.

It was these Communist ideals that inspired the Russian Revolution of 1917 and the creation of the Soviet Union, as well as the 1949 Communist Revolution in China, which heralded the People's Republic of China. However, as history shows with these two examples, despite its admirable and lofty ideals, communism on such a grand scale has proven to be far from an unshackling of chains for the oppressed proletariat. Marx would probably have turned in his Highgate grave if he knew of the atrocities carried out in the name of communism. However, many argue that communism has never been implemented in the way Marx envisioned and, as a strong antidote to capitalism, his theories are still relevant today.

# FRIEDRICH NIETZSCHE
## 1844–1900

Much of Friedrich Nietzsche's philosophical work, which considers questions of morality, religion and ethics, is controversial and open to interpretation, but his ideas attempted to break through many of the established Western philosophical views. Nietzsche introduces his radical and audacious philosophy in his 1889 book, *Twilight of the Idols or, How to Philosophize with a Hammer.* In it he takes a metaphorical hammer to philosophy and calls for a "transvaluation" or re-evaluation of societal values – an idea adopted by Postmodern theorists. Many of the themes covered in his writings were precursors of Existentialism.

Nietzsche was born near Leipzig, Germany, and his life was dogged by physical and mental illness – even as a child he was sickly. In 1849, when he was just five years old, his father (a Lutheran pastor) died, and the following year his younger brother also passed away. This early family tragedy led him to question whether there was a god, and how a god could exist in a world where such suffering existed. Despite this tragic start he later championed suffering as a force behind achievement, declaring "what does not kill me makes me stronger". Nietzsche advocated "Saying Yes to life even in its strangest and most painful episodes" (*Twilight of the Idols*). Nietzsche was influenced by the gloomy, pessimistic philosophy of **Arthur Schopenhauer** (1788–1860), and Schopenhauer's belief that the world was cruel and filled with suffering. Schopenhauer said the one thing that can relieve our suffering was art, of which music was the highest form. Being very much into music – and a friend of Richard Wagner – Nietzsche agreed.

Nietzsche developed his own individualistic philosophy that challenged accepted Christian and Utilitarian morality. Declaring that God is dead, he asked "how shall we comfort ourselves [now]?" Without a belief in the certainties of God, Nietzsche feared Europe would descend into nihilism – the belief that nothing is important in life – so he set out to overcome this. In *Thus Spoke Zarathustra* (published in four parts between 1883 and

1891) and *Beyond Good and Evil* (1886), he argued that the basic human drive is a "will to power" and that the "life-denying" "slave morality" of Christianity and liberal democracy favoured the weak and downtrodden: it allowed the weak to rule the strong. He called for a new "life-affirming" morality that accepted that there was just this one world, and that embraced life in the here and now rather than suffering in the hope of attaining access to a more perfect future world, or "heaven", as Christian morality would have people believe. Nietzsche's life-affirming philosophy championed the human instincts of power, wealth, strength and health. This is embodied in his idea of the "Ubermensch" or superman, the noble man who set his own morality, values and truths rather than having them dictated to him.

At the end of his life Nietzsche had a devastating mental breakdown, after which his works were re-edited by his sister Elisabeth who used them to bolster Nazi ideology. It is accepted that she deliberately misinterpreted his work, for he routinely condemned anti-Semitism and hated nationalism, seeing it as a form of alienation, and his philosophy is deeply individualistic. Thankfully, despite this, he would go down in history as one of the most influential philosophers, whose ideas have inspired writers and artists throughout the twentieth century.

# Twentieth-Century and Postmodern Philosophy

The Enlightenment and the Modern Age had brought about revolutions in scientific thinking, and focused attention on how societies progress and organize themselves, with an emphasis on freedom, democracy and reason. The twentieth century saw the pace of change speed up even more, with the second half of the century coming to be referred to as the Postmodern period. The outcome of much of the radical political philosophizing of the Modern period was seen in Russia's Communist Revolution and the nationalism that engulfed Europe, resulting in the two World Wars that left the world ravaged and all too aware of the horrors and brutality of extreme ideology. Examining this reality, Postmodern thinkers brought their focus back to those Enlightenment goals of freedom, democracy and reason.

Philosophy separated into two distinct camps during the twentieth century with the Anglo-American Analytic school dominating initially until the European (mostly French) Continental school came along to destabilize the establishment.

The Analytic school was characterized by its desire to make philosophy scientific. The aim was to tackle philosophical questions using mathematical logic and linguistic enquiry. Analytic philosophy originated in the corridors and lecture halls of the prestigious Cambridge and Oxford universities, with pioneering philosophers such as Bertrand Russell, Alfred North Whitehead, G. E. Moore and Ludwig Wittgenstein. They were influenced by the Vienna Circle, a group of European philosophers and scientists from the 1920s and 1930s who practised logical positivism, or logical empiricism.

These thinkers were interested in philosophical questions that could be worked out logically and verified empirically: only experience could prove or disprove any statements. They weren't really interested in the contemplation of aesthetics, ethics, metaphysics or theology; seeing as none of the questions posed in these areas of philosophy could be empirically proved to be true or false, posing the question in the first place seemed pointless. What they did focus on, though, was Linguistic philosophy (see page 164): they set about analysing language in a mathematical, logical way in order to achieve greater understanding of our thinking, and the world.

In contrast to the Analytic school of philosophy were the Continental philosophers whose influences and philosophies – German Idealism, Hegelianism, Romanticism, Existentialism, Phenomenology, Absurdism, Deconstructionism and Post-structuralism – sought to challenge and up-end dominant, institutionalized ways of thinking and doing. These schools of philosophy come under the umbrella of Continental philosophy, and they flourished in Europe throughout the twentieth century, reaching their zenith during the 1950s and 1960s. These Postmodern Continental philosophers were influenced by Marxist ideology, the goal being to return agency to the individual and to emancipate society. They rejected the view that the natural sciences were the best way to understand phenomena and drew upon historical, psychological and sociological fields of study in their work.

The ideas of **Sigmund Freud** (1856–1939), and his development of psychoanalysis in an attempt to alleviate individual human suffering, had a huge influence on

Continental philosophers. His assertion that human behaviour is not just driven by conscious awareness, but that unconscious forces are at work too, helped philosophers understand human behaviour in areas of philosophy such as Ethics, Political philosophy and Metaphysics in new ways.

Through his psychoanalysis and dream analysis, and his focus on bringing the unconscious into the conscious, Freud found that his patients understood the causes of their mental distress better and thereby gained some relief from it. Philosophers took these ideas, and his belief that individuals don't always act rationally but are driven by an unconscious we know little about, and applied it to their political and social enquiries.

Although the Analytics had the Vienna Circle, the Continentals were influenced by the Frankfurt School, a group of philosophers who critiqued postmodern societies from a Marxist perspective, using Freud's discoveries about repression, personality types and the unconscious to understand how individuals function and how societies work. Frankfurt philosophers **Max Horkheimer** and

**Theodor Adorno** looked specifically at how normal, everyday people could turn toward extreme ideology, like fascism, as they had during the Second World War.

These philosophers argued that rationality and reason, as practised by Enlightenment thinkers, had not brought about greater freedoms. Rather, societies had been manipulated into "group thinking". The rational search for, and belief in, universal truths had become the dominant way of thinking and practising philosophy, but Postmodern philosophers argued that it simply served to get people thinking in the same way as each other. Progress had ultimately caused death, destruction and a breakdown in morality – as devastatingly exemplified in the Second World War.

During the second half of the twentieth century, Continental philosophers, such as Michel Foucault and Jacques Derrida, questioned the existence of the objective truths that the Analytical philosophers claimed, and were also highly sceptical of dominant ideology. They declared that all truths were subjective and argued that knowledge and value systems were historically and culturally constructed. Truth, morality, human nature, indeed all that we know, was a construct that existed in the mind and was influenced by society and history.

These Postmodern philosophers analysed culture and society, critically evaluating the Western value system and examined the metanarratives prevalent in Western societies. "Metanarratives" are the grand, universal concepts or stories that our societies accept as true. In a postmodern, secular society the grand narrative is that science, reason and logic have all the answers.

In *The Postmodern Condition: A Report on Knowledge* (1979), critical theorist and philosopher **Jean-François Lyotard** (1924-1998) defined "postmodern" as an "incredulity toward the metanarratives", a challenging of the historical explanations and "truths" that have dominated thinking since the Enlightenment. He suggested doing away with these metanarratives, replacing them with *petit recits*, or "little", localized narratives, that allow for differences in human experience and ideas – for instance, looking at the everyday experiences of people in marginalized groups as opposed to focusing on society as a whole, or "the bigger picture".

Postmodern philosophers were Sceptics with a revisionist approach, often rejecting traditional methods and approaches. They questioned long-held accepted truths, wanting to look at *how* we know things, and *who says* this is the way to live, or how we should be. This thinking was expressed in the anti-establishment, countercultural movements and groups throughout the Western world during the 1960s and 1970s: the revolutionary civil rights movement in America, the hippy movement, the anti-war movement in Paris, the feminist movement, anti-nuclear groups and the rise of environmentalism.

# PHENOMENOLOGY

Originating from the Greek word *phainomenon*, which means appearance, Phenomenology is the examination of appearance rather than reality, more specifically the examination of the subjective lived experience. It is essentially the vision of **Edmund Husserl** (1859-1938) who, in the early 1900s, developed his theory of consciousness. Like Descartes, he started with the premise that the only thing we can be certain of is our own conscious awareness. He argued that reality consists of objects and experiences, or *phenomena*, that are perceived and interpreted by individual consciousness. For Husserl, firstly, consciousness is being conscious of experiencing *phenomena*, whether they are physical objects, thoughts, emotions or elements of our imagination; and, secondly, consciousness is intentional, or directed at those particular *phenomena*. Husserl believed that in order to understand phenomena more deeply we need to suspend judgement, biases or preconceived notions directed at those phenomena – a process called "bracketing".

**Martin Heidegger** (1889-1976), another influential Continental philosopher, and Husserl's assistant for a time, disagreed with Husserl, arguing that consciousness can never be separated from its context, and that we don't just experience life consciously but that some of what we do experience is unconscious. Heidegger's ideas influenced psychoanalysis and Existentialism.

# EXISTENTIALISM

Existentialism is a philosophical and cultural movement that gained traction in the mid-twentieth century, but has its roots in the thinking of the nineteenth-century Danish philosopher, **Søren Kierkegaard** (1813–1855) and in the thinking of Friedrich Nietzsche. With a realization that "God is dead" and morality is basically a human construct, Nietzsche saw the need for individuals to put complete faith in themselves, to choose to live their lives according to their own values and beliefs. In *Fear and Trembling* (1843), Kierkegaard acknowledged complete individual free will, but also that this frightening concept could cause deep "angst".

Existentialism embodies these ideas of free will, free choice and individual responsibility. When considering the meaning of existence without a transcendental force like God to believe in, there appears to be no purpose to life at all – human existence is just a nothingness. So, the Existentialist answer is to embrace this nothingness and make something of yourself: you are completely free to invent your life how you wish. The themes of Existentialism – boredom, the absurdities of life, alienation, freedom, nothingness, doom and gloom – are explored in the literary and philosophical works of the French Existentialists, Jean-Paul Sartre (see opposite), Simone de Beauvoir (see page 160) and Albert Camus (see page 162).

# JEAN-PAUL SARTRE
## 1905–1980

The French philosopher, writer and political activist Jean-Paul Sartre was born in Paris and brought up by his mother after his father died when he was just 15 months old. He studied philosophy at the prestigious École Normale Supérieure, where he met Simone de Beauvoir, another prominent French philosopher who was studying at the equally prestigious Sorbonne; they became lifelong romantic and intellectual partners. Sartre was a communist for much of his life and spent time with Ernesto "Che" Guevara and Fidel Castro in communist Cuba in the 1960s, actively opposing the Vietnam war. He was arrested for civil disobedience during the 1968 student uprisings in the Latin Quarter of Paris, known as the Left Bank.

Sartre was a pioneer of the Existentialist movement. He wrote influential academic works that defined Existentialism and also contributed to Phenomenology.

He is best known for his novels and plays that brought Existentialist ideas to a wider audience through real-life situations. Sartre's philosophy draws upon the Phenomenology of Husserl and Heidegger, and is set out in *Transcendence of the Ego* (1936) and *Being and Nothingness* (1943).

Central to Sartre's philosophy is the concept of free will and the responsibility that it engenders: "Man, being condemned to be free, carries the weight of the whole world on his shoulders; he is responsible for the world and for himself as a way of being" (*Being and Nothingness*, 1943). He sees any belief in determinism (the philosophical idea that events and choices are determined by previous causes) as a form of self-deception or "bad faith", believing that no individual is bound by any external value system. For Sartre, "existence precedes essence"; there is no pre-existing essence to an individual's life, he simply exists, so our choices and actions determine our essence, or who we are. Therein lies the anguish: we are completely free and wholly in control of who we are, and, if every act is determining who we are, then we need to make meaningful and authentic choices – quite a lot of pressure then! Furthermore, there are no guarantees for the outcomes of the choices we make, so we have to accept that our choices might not work out the way we expected and become accustomed to the emotions of despair and angst that accompany our awareness of an unfair, absurd world, without any certainties.

# SIMONE DE BEAUVOIR
## 1908–1986

Simone de Beauvoir was a French writer, political activist and Existentialist feminist philosopher who was one of the most important figures in the feminism movement, and contributed enormously to the development of Existentialism. She studied philosophy at the Sorbonne and became the ninth woman to ever be awarded a degree there. She was the lifelong companion of fellow philosopher Jean-Paul Sartre, both influencing each other's work.

Like Sartre and Albert Camus, de Beauvoir expressed her philosophy through her novels, as well as through her essays and non-fiction works. Her major work was an exploration of Existentialist feminism – *The Second Sex* (1949). She started with the Existentialist premise that existence precedes essence, but gave it a feminist slant: "One is not born but becomes a woman." She distinguished between sex and gender, and argued that women's gender is a social and historical construct that has been defined in relation to men. Taking a historical perspective, she argued that men throughout history have made women "the other" in relation to men.

She maintained that women should shake off the stereotypes and constraints imposed upon them, reject the myth of "the eternal female" (the philosophical principle that women have an idealized, unalterable core essence that is different to men's), or what it means to be a woman, and, like true Existentialists, assert their free will, individual choice and complete authority to become what and who they are.

Simone de Beauvoir's philosophical ideas, feminist writings and political activism have inspired the second, third and fourth waves of the feminist movement, and continue to influence contemporary culture. Her Existential maxim, "Change your life today. Don't gamble on the future, act now, without delay," encourages us all to stride boldly down our own authentic path.

# ALBERT CAMUS
## 1913–1960

Though he never labelled himself as a philosopher, the French writer and political and social activist, Albert Camus, would prove to be an enormous influence on the philosophical schools of Existentialism, Absurdism and Anarchism. He was born in French Algeria and, after his father died during the First World War, he was brought up by his mother in very basic, poor conditions. Despite such a challenging start in life, he went on to study philosophy at the University of Algiers and was awarded the Nobel Prize in Literature when he was aged 44, but he tragically died in a car accident two years later.

Although he never accepted that he was a philosopher, let alone an Existentialist, his writing focused on the Existentialist notion of the meaninglessness of existence, and how individuals should embrace that meaninglessness and not try to escape it by looking to outside sources such as religion; that would be entering into "bad faith"

or "philosophical suicide". He believed the philosophical question, "What is the meaning of existence?", was unanswerable and that we simply have to live with the paradox that we will always seek an answer to this question yet never find it, a concept known as "the absurd". He advocated living life intensely, in the present, and letting our conscious awareness of the absurd and our mortality lead to a greater appreciation of life.

# LINGUISTIC PHILOSOPHY

Linguistic philosophy tries to solve philosophical problems by looking to understand more about the language we use. **Gottlob Frege** (1848-1925), a German mathematician and philosopher, turned his attention to language and the importance of meaning and definition in his 1892 essay "On Sense and Reference". He distinguished between the "sense" of a word or object – what we mean by our words, which can be subjective and varies from person to person – and the "referent", or what a word is actually referring to. He concluded that words can be defined by their context in a sentence.

**Bertrand Russell** (1872-1970) developed Frege's ideas, and his works put language at the heart of how we approach philosophy. Russell was a mathematician and logician and one of Britain's most famous twentieth-century philosophers. In his essay *On Denoting*, published in 1905, he set out to analyse the grammar and syntax we use and ensure that our language is logically clear in order that we can work out philosophical truths and falsities.

Russell's student and friend **Ludwig Wittgenstein** (1889–1951) developed Frege's ideas, saying that objectively defining words is a difficult business, because someone can always come up with a counterexample; I might have one idea about what "friendship" entails, but my friend may have a completely different one. He said we define the meaning of words by *using* them publicly in our communities. He accepted that words and meanings change over time and with different people, and he also pointed out that there is always the risk of differences in meaning between what the speaker intends and how the audience understands it. Wittgenstein says confusion occurs when language is used outside its original context. People can become "bewitched by language". He highlighted philosophical problems as being the biggest culprits of this wordplay – questions like "What is truth?" simply serve to confuse – and he encouraged philosophers to "bring words back from their metaphysical to their everyday use" as part of an idea that became known as "ordinary language philosophy".

# STRUCTURALISM AND POST-STRUCTURALISM

Structuralism was a twentieth-century intellectual movement in France that sought to uncover and examine the hidden patterns or structures underlying cultural phenomena such as the family, political systems, fashion, art or literature. The idea was to take a particular aspect of culture (mythological stories, for example), and, by breaking that aspect down into its individual components and subcomponents (the events in the story) and analyzing those parts, Structuralists said we can identify the "structures" that can be found in all myths across cultures.

**Claude Lévi-Strauss** (1908–2009) – not the creator of hard-wearing, cool jeans but the French anthropologist who was a key figure in the development of Structuralism – analysed the relationships between the individual components of myths. He called them "mythemes", and found out things like: all myths deal with the tension between binary opposites – good versus evil, selfishness versus altruism, and so on. Lévi-Strauss was influenced by the Swiss linguistic theorist **Ferdinand de Saussure** (1857–1913), who came up with a science of signs called semiotics and said that language is a system, or structure, made up of binary opposites; we understand what white is because we contrast it with black. It was this scientific approach to the study of society that Structuralists were aiming for, uncovering universal rules.

Post-structuralists of the mid-twentieth century saw Structuralism as too rigid, and doubted the existence of universal cultural rules, arguing instead that ideas, our realities and our studies of underlying structures have been influenced by history and culture. Post-structuralist French philosophers such as Michel Foucault (see page 170) and Jacques Derrida (see page 172) argued that one must examine each cultural phenomenon itself as well as the context within which it was produced. Post-structuralism asserts that meanings are forever shifting and that everything has multiple meanings depending on the intent of the producer and the interpretation of the observer.

# MICHEL FOUCAULT
## 1926–1984

Michel Foucault was a French Continental philosopher, sociologist and radical political activist. In his young adulthood he suffered with terrible depression and had a preoccupation with suicide, attempting it himself many times. This led him to study psychology and philosophy at the Parisian École Normale Supérieure. He is grouped with the Post-structuralists, but he considered his work a historical critique of Modernity, an examination of how all knowledge is linked to power, and how this interaction between knowledge and power influences human beings.

By looking at the power relations prevalent in society, Foucault showed how authority is used to discipline and control people – we bow down to the authority of the physician or psychiatrist. His work analysed power relations in areas of law and punishment, the police, sexuality, psychiatry and modern medicine, and argued that modern ways of treating the mentally ill, criminals, patients and how we view our sexuality are not necessarily an improvement on those of the past. He was inspired by Nietzsche, particularly the belief that studying history should be all about informing us how we can live better lives now.

In 1961 he published his famous work *Madness and Civilization*, which looks back to the Renaissance as a "Golden Age" for people with mental illnesses, as they were not locked up and stigmatized at that time. Rather, they were seen merely as being different and possessing their own kind of wisdom. Foucault's *Madness and Civilization* got society questioning what constitutes madness and how we treat mental illness. He took the Post-structuralist approach of not only looking at the prevailing or privileged ideas but also the subordinate, overlooked ones, and, by making historical comparisons, he asked: Are we really doing things better now?

# JACQUES DERRIDA
## 1930–2004

Jacques Derrida was an influential member of the twentieth-century French philosophy scene and was the founder of Deconstructionism. Born in Algeria (like Albert Camus), he studied philosophy at – yes, you guessed it – the illustrious École Normale Supérieure in the 1950s, where he encountered Michel Foucault, and later at Harvard. He went on to teach philosophy at his alma mater as well as the Sorbonne, and taught at various prestigious universities in America. He wrote prolifically (averaging more than one published work a year from 1972 onwards) but was often criticized for his pretentious and obscure writing style; nonetheless he challenged established ideas and had a huge impact on contemporary literary theory and Continental philosophy.

His early philosophy was influenced by the Phenomenologist, Edmund Husserl, as well as Martin Heidegger, Friedrich Nietzsche and Sigmund Freud.

He criticized the simplicity of Phenomenology and Structuralism, and is seen as an architect in the development of Post-structuralism.

He set out his concept of Deconstructionism in his books *Of Grammatology, Speech and Phenomena* and *Writing and Difference*, all published in 1967. Deconstructionism is a theory of literary criticism and a way of approaching philosophy that deconstruct thinking and ideas. Drawing from Structuralism's theory of binary opposition (we understand things based on their relationship with an opposite, so we know what good means by comparing it to evil), he argues that all our thinking focuses on a privileged idea at the expense of an overlooked opposite. For example: reason is regarded more highly than passion, high culture is privileged over low culture, and speech over writing. To deconstruct is to turn our gaze toward the opposites, be curious about the subservient concepts in order to improve our understanding of the whole.

This act of deconstruction exposes the faults in our thinking and can cause confusion, highlighting the uncertainty in our ideas, but Derrida said we should embrace this confusion as a state of *aporia*, the Ancient Greek word meaning "puzzlement" or "impasse". Derrida felt that rather than feeling insecure or fearful we should feel comfortable in the knowledge that, often, there are no perfect solutions to the philosophical questions we have about life.

# Philosophy Today

So where are we now with philosophy? Are we any closer to those perfect answers Derrida and the Continental philosophers of the twentieth century said were unattainable? Has contemporary society thrown up new questions for philosophers to try to solve?

When Descartes proclaimed, in the seventeenth century, "I think, therefore I am", he identified the mind with consciousness, distinguishing it from the brain and adding dualism to the age-old mind–body problem. Fast forward to today, as science advances and neuroscience makes great leaps forward in our understanding of the brain and how it works, the problem of consciousness is still being explored.

**David Chalmers** (1966–), the Australian philosopher and cognitive scientist, coined the phrase the "hard problem" of consciousness: Why do we have subjective experiences of consciousness? We know what happens in the brain physically – we can see that in brain scans – but the "hard problem" is how we explain why we each have our own "inner movie" going, which allows us to see and experience the world around us. Why aren't we all walking around like robots?

This brings us to another pressing philosophical area of enquiry: artificial intelligence (AI) and the conundrums it raises around consciousness and our relationship with advancing technologies. If consciousness has a universal quality and can be found in everything to varying degrees (something Chalmers considered), what are the ethical implications for AI? If we can create technologies that have human-like comprehension and agency, do they have rights like humans? Or, as the philosopher **Daniel Dennett** (1942–) suggests, should we just keep them in their place and not attribute human characteristics to them, as they are, after all, simply machines?

As technological advances in artificial intelligence move toward creating human-like robots, we find ourselves asking, What defines a "person"? In a world where all aspects of our biological, psychological and genetic make-up can be manipulated, that question becomes ever more complex.

The Post-Structuralist, political and feminist philosopher, **Judith Butler** (1956–) explores an aspect of this in her work on gender performativity. In *Gender Trouble*, she suggests we know how to be female or male because we constantly perform acts that are in keeping with these genders. By copying and repeating the *actions* of being female or male we *become* female or male. She challenges the concept of binary sex (that human beings are naturally one of two sexes) and has been hugely influential in contemporary feminist and Queer theory as well as Ethics.

As more and more women appear on the philosophical scene, one hopes that after thousands of years of male dominance we will see a future where Western philosophy is more inclusive and representative of society as a whole. Indeed, philosophers from all over the world are now part of the philosophical conversation, forging the path for a more "global" philosophy.

How can philosophy in the twenty-first century help us lead better lives? For **Alain de Botton** (1969–), the Swiss-born British philosopher and writer, philosophy can help us understand ourselves and each other better and can be used as a therapeutic tool. In *The Consolations of Philosophy* (2000), he explores how turning to the great philosophers – Socrates, Epicurus,

Nietzsche, Schopenhauer and Seneca – can console us in times of difficulty, when we feel inadequate or unpopular, when we feel we haven't enough money, or when we have a broken heart. In 2008, he co-founded The School of Life, an educational company that provides a forum for people to explore life's issues with the help of philosophy.

Like all the periods in history we have discussed in this little book, the twenty-first century needs radical thinkers with radical ideas. As we have seen, philosophers throughout time have upset the apple cart: they have been excommunicated for their ideas; they have been banished or sent to prison; some, like poor Socrates, have even been killed because their ideas have taken our understanding of human life and the world around us in a completely novel direction. In a world where a mass of information and misinformation is at our fingertips, we need philosophical enquiry more than ever. Asking and exploring big questions, being filled with curiosity and wonder about life – these are the things that lie at the heart of philosophy.

# Five Philosophical Questions

As we said at the beginning of this little book, the aim of philosophy is to ask and explore life's big questions in order to improve our lives or aid "flourishing", the lovely term philosophers use when talking about living a good life. To flourish is to live life to the full and experience positive emotions, psychological well-being and social happiness most of the time. Flourishing and happiness are what Aristotle was searching for with his concept of *eudaimonia*. Aristotle said the aim of practical philosophy was to find out how *eudaimonia* can be achieved and, as we have explored in this book, for thousands of years philosophers have tried to provide answers to these big questions, answers that can help humans flourish. Over the final few pages we will briefly explore five of the big questions and see what philosophers have made of them over the years. But then it's over to you: how can philosophy help you flourish and what will you ask of life?

# WHO AM I?

What makes us who we are? Are we what we think, feel, reflect upon, remember?

Are we just a physical being of around a hundred trillion cells functioning like a machine, even our mental output, as the Materialists would have us believe? Or, do we have a mind that operates in a completely different way to our body – the Cartesian dualism of mind and body as Descartes suggests? The mind–body problem still perplexes philosophers today.

If we go with Cartesian dualism and believe that the mind or mental perceptions exist outside the material body, then we have the possibility of each of us having a soul. Aristotle believed the mind, or soul, is the essence of any living thing; and many religions believe the soul lives on when the body dies, so this soul, mind, spirit or consciousness, as we call it, must be different to our physical bodies, right?

Each of us is an ever-changing mix of physical qualities and mental perceptions, our emotional and psychological being; all that we think, feel, remember, imagine and do contribute to making us who we are.

For **Gilbert Ryle** (1900–1976), the British philosopher who critiqued Cartesian dualism, human consciousness and the mind are completely dependent upon the human brain, and the idea of a soul or mind is scientifically unfounded and simply "the ghost in the machine". As our understanding about how the brain works improves through advances in neuroscience, our ideas about what makes us *who we are*, are constantly evolving.

# WHAT IS RIGHT AND WRONG?

So, who decides what is right and wrong? And are *they* right? For thousands of years societies have based their morality on religious edicts. For example, Christianity and Judaism have the ten commandments, which dictate the right and wrong ways to behave. In the majority of modern, secular societies we have rules and laws that govern right and wrong actions. Some philosophers, called Ethical Intuitionists, think that the majority of humans intuitively know what is right and wrong: "moral truths" exist outside our decision making so do we really need laws or rules?

The field of ethics concerns decisions about what is right and wrong, which can be reached by rigorously examining moral principles and ethical problems, such as: Is it always right that we must not kill? Is abortion wrong? Is it right to eat meat? Individuals and communities will have different responses based on their own biases and beliefs, so the objective moral truths are impossible to ascertain. Determining what is right and wrong is ultimately always influenced by history, culture, political power, religion, human conscience and a desire to do what is right and good.

# FREE WILL OR DETERMINISM?

To have free will is to be free to act without fate or necessity getting in the way. Determinism, on the other hand, states that all actions and events are determined by external forces. When we make choices, especially the big life-changing ones, are we free to choose? Or are there outside forces at work that determine what we can do with our lives? Have these outside forces – the political system we are living under, the genetic make-up we have inherited, forces of fate or maybe an omniscient god – decreed all our actions in advance? Has the economic or social class into which we were born determined the route we take in life? Or are we all completely free to do whatever we want? John Locke believed free will was an illusion, and he illustrated this with the story of a man who is carried into a room while asleep and then locked in. When he wakes, he chooses to stay put without knowing he actually cannot leave. If he chooses to leave, he will realize he is not free to choose at all: the locked door has determined the outcome of his action. If Locke is right, if we don't have free will and all our actions are determined by forces beyond our control, can we be held morally responsible for our actions?

Some philosophers suggest that, in life, we exist between both free will and determinism. According to the Stoics, the key is to exert your will as freely as you can and accept that you might come up against situations that determine your choices. The important thing is to take responsibility for your life as far as you can.

# WHAT HAPPENS AFTER DEATH?

The question of whether something of us survives after death is one of life's great questions, and philosophers have been coming up with ideas about it for thousands of years. The Ancient philosophers, Socrates and Plato, believed the soul lived on after the death of the body, however Epictetus argued that when the body dies the soul, or the mind, simply ceases to exist. Both theories seek to soothe the fear of death or to allay the incomprehensible concept that once we are dead there is nothing.

Theistic theories of life after death range from the Buddhist concept of reincarnation and the ultimate post-death goal of nirvana to the Christian ideas of heaven and hell. Hindus believe the soul or *atman* leaves the body and reincarnates itself, while Muslims believe in a paradise (*Jannah*) and a hell (*Jahannam*). Tied to these concepts of life after death are beliefs that if people do the right thing and believe in God in this life, they will go on to a better afterlife.

But, can it be empirically proven? The answer is a categorical no. Neuroscientists taking a Physicalist (everything is physical, nothing exists beyond the physical) stance say that consciousness is a result of neurons firing around the brain, and so, when the brain dies, the activity that creates the mind dies too. Whichever theory is true, it's really not worth worrying about, as Marcus Aurelius, that great Roman Stoic, said in *Meditations*: "It is not death that a man should fear, but he should fear never beginning to live."

# WHAT IS THE MEANING OF LIFE?

For many people the meaning of life can be found in spiritual or religious contemplation. For thousands of years people looked to their gods, or their spiritual leaders or gurus, for how to live their lives and what it was all about: follow the word of the Lord and therein you will find life's meaning. But Nietzsche's declaration that "God is dead" and the idea of survival of the fittest, which emerged from the scientific revolution, began to suggest that the meaning of life might be simply the propagation of the species, and ideas about life having any kind of meaning at all were thrown into disarray.

Life, as Camus said, can appear pretty absurd and meaningless – but we can face the absurdity and live life to the full, with passion and authenticity. The realization that life has no objective meaning means that it is up to you to decide what your strong reason for living is. It could be connecting with other people and creating wonderful, loving family relationships and friendships, or realizing your full potential, pursuing wisdom and knowledge and fulfilling your dreams. You may find a deep sense of meaning in nature or making art or serving others. We may just be tiny specks in a vast universe but within our own little space in time we are hugely significant.

# Further Reading

If you've enjoyed this book and would like to read more about the topics covered, these books are a great place to start:

## INTRODUCTIONS AND GENERAL

*History of Western Philosophy,* Bertrand Russell (1945)
*The Consolations of Philosophy,* Alain de Botton (2000)
*Philosophy for Life and Other Dangerous Situations,* Jules Evans (2012)
*Philosophy: The Basics,* Nigel Warburton (2007)
*Philosophy 1: A Guide Through the Subject,* A. C. Grayling (1995)
*Justice: What's the Right Thing to Do?* Michael J. Sandel (2009)
*Brainstorms,* Daniel Dennett (1981)

## NOVELS

*Zen and the Art of Motorcycle Maintenance,* Robert Pirsig (1974)
*Sophie's World,* Jostein Gaarder (1991)
*The Outsider,* Albert Camus (1942)
*She Came to Stay,* Simone de Beauvoir (1943)
*Thus Spoke Zarathustra,* Friedrich Nietzsche (1883–1891)